Describing Spoken English

"This excellent book offers unmatched coverage of all aspects of English pronunciation, including stress and intonation."

Larry Trask, *University of Sussex*

Describing Spoken English provides a practical and descriptive introduction to the pronunciation of contemporary English. It requires no prior knowledge of phonetics or phonology.

Charles W. Kreidler examines the main varieties of English in the world today. He focuses on the elements common to all native-speaker varieties of English and presents the differences as minor variations on a theme.

The book is divided into twelve chapters which cover the following subjects:

- speech production
- principles of phonological analysis
- consonants
- the vowel systems of different varieties of the language
- syllable structure
- strong and weak syllables
- phonological processes in connected speech
- stress in simple words and compounds
- tone units and utterances
- the role of accent in discourse
- intonation and rhythm
- the interrelations of morphology and phonology

Each topic is presented in an accessible, jargon-free style. Chapters are clearly structured, with summaries, bibliographies, and exercises to encourage active participation.

This textbook will be essential reading for undergraduate and post-graduate students of English language and linguistics.

Charles W. Kreidler is Emeritus Professor of Linguistics at Georgetown University. His publications include *The Dynamics of Language* (1971) and *The Pronunciation of English* (1989).

ROUTLEDGE

LONDON AND NEW YORK

Describing

Spoken

English

An introduction

Charles W. Kreidler

ROUTLEDGE

First published 1997
by Routledge
11 New Fetter Lane, London EC4P 4EE

Simultaneously published in the USA
and Canada
by Routledge 29 West 35th Street,
New York, NY 10001

Typeset in Times by Keystroke,
Jacaranda Lodge, Wolverhampton

Printed and bound in Great Britain by
Hartnolls Limited, Bodmin, Cornwall

*British Library Cataloguing in
Publication Data*
A catalogue record for this book is
available from the British Library

*Library of Congress Cataloguing in
Publication Data*
Kreidler, Charles W., 1924–
    Describing spoken English: an
introduction / Charles Kreidler.
    Includes bibliographical references
and index.
    1. English language – Spoken
English.   2. English language –
Variation.   3. Linguistics.   I. Title.
PE1074.8.K74 1997
421'.52—dc20   96–9601

ISBN 0–415–15094–9 (hbk)
ISBN 0–415–15095–7 (pbk)

For Carol

Contents

Preface   xi
Symbols and typographic conventions   xii

1 The pronunciation of English   1

1.1 Dialects   2
1.2 English outside of England   5
1.3 Differences and commonalities   7
1.4 Plan of this book   9

2 Speech   13

2.1 The nature of sound   14
2.2 Speech   16
2.3 Consonants   18
2.4 Vowels   26
2.5 Syllables and prosodic features   29

3 The structure of language   33

3.1 Units of language   34
3.2 Knowing one's native language   37
3.3 Phonemes   39

4 English consonants 49

4.1 Distinctive features 50
4.2 Consonant allophones 56

5 English vowels 65

5.1 Dialect differences 66
5.2 A general inventory of vowels 69
5.3 Vowel inventories of specific English dialects 80

6 Syllables 85

6.1 The structure of a syllable 87
6.2 Consonants in clusters 90
6.3 Inflections 96

7 Strong and weak syllables 101

7.1 Accent and stress 102
7.2 Weak syllables 109
7.3 Variation in weak syllables 112

8 Word stress 123

8.1 The phonological structure of words: stress patterns 124
8.2 The morphological structure of words 130
8.3 Rules for stress in simple words 135

9 Stress in compound words and phrases 143

9.1 Noun phrases and noun compounds 144
9.2 Adjective and adverb constructions 149
9.3 Compounds in phrases and larger compounds 152
9.4 Verb phrases and verb compounds 154

10 The role of accent in discourse 161

10.1 The structure of a tone unit 162
10.2 Tonality 164
10.3 Tonicity 166

11 Intonation 177

11.1 Paralanguage 178
11.2 Intonations of the simple tone unit 180
11.3 Low and high onsets 186
11.4 Compound tunes 187

12 Morphemes that vary in form 195

12.1 Phonologically conditioned alternations 197
12.2 Morphological conditioning 200
12.3 Another past tense suffix 206

Feedback on exercises 212
Bibliography 225
Index 231

Preface

This is a description of present-day English pronunciation. It aims to describe the principal native-speaker varieties of English, showing the phonological elements shared by all varieties of the language and setting out specific differences against a framework of commonality. The book is intended to be a text for undergraduate and postgraduate students whose field of study includes linguistics and/or English language, and for those who are preparing to teach English as a second or foreign language. It should be useful to both native speakers and those who have acquired the language through formal instruction.

I assume no previous knowledge of phonetic description or phonological principles, which are introduced in the second and third chapters, respectively. I have tried to make the book a useful tool for learning by providing an abundance of data – words, phrases, sentences – and exercises that call on students to participate continually in the development of topics, mainly by leading them to examine their own pronunciation.

I am grateful to anonymous readers of the manuscript for valuable suggestions and to the staff of Routledge for their expert care in turning the manuscript into a book. Responsibility for the contents rests with me, of course.

C.W.K.

Symbols and typographic conventions

Every academic discipline has its own technical terminology, and a book like this one also requires special symbols to indicate features of the spoken language. The terms and symbols used in this text are explained as they are introduced, but an overall account of them here may be useful.

All technical terms appear in **bold type** when they first occur or are discussed in detail, and all are listed in the Index.

To describe pronunciation we need examples of **utterances**, relatively short, meaningful stretches of speech that have been produced or might be produced by some speaker of English and understood by other speakers of the language. Such utterances appear frequently in this text and are always within double quotation marks (" . . . "). In addition, we often cite words, phrases, and sentences that illustrate some particular point. These are in italics when they are part of the running text – part of a paragraph – but are in ordinary type when they appear in columns apart from the running text.

Chapter 2, introducing the elements of phonetics, uses the symbols of the International Phonetic Alphabet for speech sounds, each symbol enclosed in square brackets. In Chapter 3, dealing with the sound system of English, the IPA symbols, somewhat modified, appear within slant lines to indicate the phonemes of English.

Chapter 5 introduces twenty-four key words, each of which has a different vowel and stands for all the words that might contain that vowel. These are in small capitals (CHICK, STEP, BAT, etc.).

In Chapter 5 we also introduce the use of acute (´) and grave (`) accent marks over vowel letters to indicate different degrees of syllable prominence. Beginning with Chapter 8 arrows, ↑ and ↓, are used to show rising and falling intonation, respectively. Chapter 11 introduces more diacritics for intonation: ↗ for a short rise, ↘ for a short fall, circumflex (ˆ) for rise–fall, caron (ˇ) for fall–rise, and a small raised circle (°) for high onset.

Chapter 1

The pronunciation of English

- **1.1 Dialects**   2
- **1.2 English outside of England**   5
- **1.3 Differences and commonalities**   7
- **1.4 Plan of this book**   9

The purpose of this book, as the title suggests, is to describe how English is pronounced by native speakers of the language. Native speakers now number approximately 350 million and they live in widely separated parts of the world. There are differences in the way these people speak English, of course, but the varieties are mutually intelligible to a high degree: Australians understand Canadians and vice versa, Londoners and New Yorkers, residents of Dublin and Johannesburg communicate successfully.

1.1 Dialects

When people who have the same native language can understand one another and at the same time notice consistent differences in each other's speech, we say that they speak different **dialects** of the same language. The term 'dialect' is, unfortunately, not a very precise one. Any two people have differences in their way of talking. How different must ways of speaking be in order for us to call them different dialects? Professional linguists who specialize in dialectology use various criteria of pronunciation, vocabulary, or grammatical expressions to make a distinction between one dialect area of a country and another dialect area, but no one assumes that the way of speaking is completely uniform within a single dialect area.

Any language that has a large number of speakers develops variation in the ways that people use that language, especially if there are barriers that make frequent communication difficult. One kind of barrier is geographic – mountains, swamps, oceans, or simply distance. Up until modern times few people ever went far from the place where they were born and had little to do with others who lived, say, fifty miles away or less; or, if they migrated to another area, they moved just once and stayed where they settled. Thus in England there were once rather numerous regional dialects reflecting the feudal society of the Middle Ages, and these have by no means disappeared. Today there is still a distinction between Northern and Southern dialects. One prominent feature distinguishing the two is that Northern speakers pronounce *nut*, *some*, *young*, for example, with the same vowel sound as in *put*, *bush*, *full*, whereas these are two distinct vowels in Southern pronunciation – and in the rest of the English-speaking world. (There is something more about this matter in Chapter 5.)

Today more people are able to travel back and forth without migrating, and in our times communication does not require face-to-face exchanges. Through cinema, radio, and television we are constantly exposed to voices from far away. We understand what we hear even while noting differences of pronunciation or word usage, and in time we take these differences for granted. However, we should note that the media – or at least the producers of radio and television programs that are broadcast nationally and internationally – do a certain amount of editing; they eliminate linguistic features that have only local acceptance. Thus they contribute to the establishment of usage that is supradialectal.

While such forces are at work to promote greater uniformity, other forces pull in the opposite direction. Humans form social bonds. Two small examples of social differentiation are sex and age: men and women use different speech forms, and each generation of adolescents introduces new words and new meanings for old words, which distinguish their way of talking from that of their elders. More relevant in a discussion of dialectology is the fact that complex societies consist of several groups, perhaps overlapping, distinguished from one another on the basis of wealth, education, occupations, ethnicity, religion, or some combination of these. In varying degrees people want to be identified as belonging to specific groups. Some individuals aim for 'upward mobility' and try to imitate those who seem to be better off; others want to promote the 'upward mobility' of the group they already belong to; still others have no desire for change of any kind but want to maintain whatever keeps their group separate from others. Group identification can take the form of some common preference in clothing, jewelry, vehicles, mannerisms, or way of talking. Recent investigations in Glasgow, Liverpool, Philadelphia, Toronto, and Sydney, among other large cities, have shown the growth and spread of indigenous language forms among such groups.

Variation in language is not only a matter of geographic and social dialects. All of us vary in what we say in a range from the most

3

formal situations to the most casual, depending on the situation and the people we are conversing with. In Chapter 7 we consider how faster, more casual speech differs from more formal pronunciations. And written language – especially printed language – is unlike most speech. Speakers, in conversations or in more formal addresses, can usually find out what their listeners know and aim their words accordingly, and they can correct themselves if necessary; some of what is communicated will be in the speaker's tone of voice and in the situation where speaking is going on. Authors of written material, on the other hand, have to exercise more care with each sentence, not knowing what they can count on their intended audience to supply.

Discussion of dialects frequently leads to the question of a **standard** (or standards), a term which, like 'dialect,' is easily tossed around in ordinary conversation but not so easily defined for serious descriptive work. Just as producers of radio and television programs today may filter out the language forms that are local in order to gain wide acceptance for their productions, in a similar way publishers of books and newspapers began centuries ago to establish standards for grammar and spelling. Along with the need, or desirability, of some standardization goes the matter of prestige. In making choices among forms that were in current use, publishers quite naturally chose the usage of the upper classes. So the standard for written English is essentially based on the dialect of London as spoken by members of 'the Establishment.' For written English, notice. A prestige way of speaking, based on the same upper-class dialect, has come to be called Received Pronunciation (generally abbreviated as RP). RP now typifies the speech of educated people, not restricted to any particular area of England. Until recently all voices heard on the British Broadcasting Corporation spoke RP, and RP has been the form of English taught to foreigners wherever British influence has been strong. For all that, less than 5 percent of the English population speak it.

The distinction between Northern and Southern dialects in England has been mentioned. Within these broad divisions urban varieties, quite distinct in character, can be noted; for example, Liverpool, Birmingham, Manchester, Norwich. London not only gave birth to the standard form of English but is also the home of Cockney, the dialect associated with the working classes of that city.

4

1.2 English outside of England

English has been spoken in Wales since the Norman Conquest, and Wales has been politically united with England since the middle of the sixteenth century. Since then, and especially with the advent of industrialization in the early nineteenth century, English has become dominant over the Welsh language. However, there are strong efforts today to keep the latter alive by promoting bilingualism.

When Scotland became united with England in the seventeenth century, the lowlands of that country were inhabited by people speaking Scots, which, depending on one's viewpoint, is either a dialect of English or a closely related language. Speakers of Scots Gaelic peopled the highlands and outer islands. Scots Gaelic has all but disappeared. The language now spoken throughout Scotland is clearly English (though many Scots would refuse to call it so), but it is also clearly a form different from that spoken in England, with a great deal of distinctive vocabulary and a pronunciation distinct from that of RP.

Ireland, the island, is two separate political entities and two rather different dialect areas. Ulster, or Northern Ireland, is part of the United Kingdom. The speech of many of its inhabitants is close to that of Scotland in pronunciation since their ancestors came from there in the seventeenth century. The original inhabitants of what is now the Republic of Ireland spoke Irish Gaelic, and Irish English has been influenced by that language.

Wales, Scotland, and the Republic of Ireland show considerable linguistic diversity throughout their respective territories but there are no clear dialect boundaries within those territories. It should be pointed out here that Scottish English and Irish English retain features that have been lost in RP – the pronunciation of R in words like *car* and *card*, for example.

English has been spoken in North America (Canada and the United States) since the beginning of the seventeenth century. In both countries the original settlements by colonists from the British Isles have been augmented by migrants from other parts of the world, who – or whose children – learned English in the new world. In Canada the island province of Newfoundland has had a separate history from the rest of the country and forms a dialect area apart. So too do the maritime provinces (Nova Scotia, New Brunswick, and Prince Edward Island), the area of earliest settlement on the mainland by speakers of English. The rest of the country shows – or is said to show – remarkable linguistic uniformity for so large a country.

The dialect situation in the United States is somewhat similar: fairly clear dialect areas on the east coast and greater homogeneity as one goes west, reflecting the separate settlement of the original colonies and the mixing of populations in their westward movements. A Northern dialect area includes all New England, New York, and northern New Jersey, then stretches westward across the Great Lakes and along the Canadian border to the Pacific coast. A Southern dialect area begins in Delaware and Maryland and extends on the eastern side of the Appalachian Mountains to Florida, then westward along the Gulf coast to southern Texas. The remainder, called the Midland area, includes only Pennsylvania and New Jersey on the Atlantic coast but, past the Appalachians, expands to include nearly all the country. What is sometimes called 'General American' is a Midland dialect.

English is spoken in and around the Caribbean Sea: Bermuda in the Atlantic Ocean; Belize in Central America, Guyana in South America, and the Bahamas, Jamaica, the Virgin Islands, St Kitts, Nevis, Monserrat, Anguilla, Antigua, Dominica, St Lucia, Barbados, St Vincent, Grenada, and Trinidad and Tobago. In this area it was first established as the masters' language, serving as the only means of communication among a population of slaves forcibly carried from West Africa to the insular and litoral plantations engaged in producing a single crop (monocultivation). As first established, the language used was a pidgin – a simplified form of the language of the dominant social group. When a pidgin has been learned by a generation of children, it expands greatly and becomes a creole. In the Caribbean area today there are varieties of English ranging from standard forms of English to creoles, which are not comprehensible to speakers of a standard form. (There are also creoles of French, Spanish, Dutch, and Portuguese.)

Australia, where English colonization began at the end of the eighteenth century, is quite uniform linguistically. It has vocabulary items which are uniquely Australian, drawn mainly from the languages spoken there indigenously, but its close ties to Britain and the recency of settlement keep it linguistically close. Pronunciation ranges from RP to something close to 'Broad Australian,' which has similarities with Cockney.

English and Scottish settlement of New Zealand dates only from the 1820s and, except that South Island supposedly shows more Scottish influence than North Island, there is not much linguistic diversity within the country. As with Australia, there are words in use that are not known elsewhere (borrowed from Maori) but British English has been the model of prestige in other matters of usage.

Only 10 percent of South Africa's population speak English as a native language, but English is the preferred language in business, education, journalism, and public life generally. Thus linguistic differences among South Africans who are native speakers of English are not great, but the English spoken by members of other ethnic groups for whom it is a second language, shows great diversity. Among native speakers, Broad South African shows interesting differences of pronunciation from the English spoken elsewhere in the world. Chapter 5 has some notes on these distinctive traits.

While this book can deal only with native-speaker varieties of English, it would be wrong not to take notice of the fact that it is an important language for commerce, education, and administration – even having status as the official language or one of the official languages – in countries which have no large population of native English-speakers. Apart from Liberia and the Philippines, which have been influenced by American English, these countries are territories of the former British Empire, now independent, whether members of the Commonwealth or not. Naturally English becomes somewhat different in the various places where it is spoken, under the influence of these different native languages. So the plural term 'New Englishes' is appropriate for the kinds of English that are developing in South Asia (India, Pakistan, Bangladesh, Sri Lanka), Southeast Asia (Singapore, Malaysia, Hong Kong), West Africa (Nigeria, Ghana, Sierra Leone, Gambia, Cameroon), and East Africa (Kenya, Uganda, Tanzania, Zambia, Malawi, and Zimbabwe).

1.3 Differences and commonalities

If speakers of different dialects communicate successfully while noticing differences in each other's way of talking, then obviously what they have in common, linguistically, is much more than what they do not share. What has to be alike and what can be different?

When we listen to people who come from a dialect area different from our own, we notice the ways in which their speech differs from ours. The most striking things may not be part of language itself but rather certain characteristics of their delivery – speaking fast or slowly, in a shrill voice or a hoarse one, in a monotone or with a wide range of pitch. These features of speech are called **paralanguage**; they occur in speech and they may influence our impression of the speaker and therefore our interpretation of what the speaker says, but they are not part of language: they do not communicate anything in themselves. Section 11.1 deals with paralanguage.

We may notice that other speakers use words that we do not use or use them with different meanings than what we give them (vocabulary differences). Differences of vocabulary can lead to misunderstandings, but misunderstandings arise among people who know each other well, who live together. Speakers may use different word forms, for example, *dove* or *dived* as the past of *dive*, *got* or *gotten* as the past participle of *get* (differences of morphology). It is possible that we will observe a difference in the way words are put together to express a meaning (differences in syntax), but syntactic differences in English are very slight. Do you say "He gave it me" or "He gave me it"? "I looked out the window" or "I looked out of the window"? Perhaps we would not even recognize that we had heard something unfamiliar.

So far as pronunciation is concerned, we may notice features of intonation; perhaps the speaker seems to go up at the end of an utterance where we would expect the voice to fall, or vice versa. But this in itself points to a commonality: speakers of English – and apparently of all languages – speak in melodies that are meaningful. We notice an intonational difference only because we take the familiar, identical intonations for granted.

We are most likely to notice when the pronunciation of a specific word is different from what we would say; perhaps the speaker stresses a different syllable of the word. But this is possible only because of the nature of the English language. In some languages – Chinese, Thai, Vietnamese, for example – most words are one syllable long. English has numerous monosyllabic words but also many polysyllabic ones. In some languages with polysyllabic words, such as Czech and Polish, the stressed syllable always occupies the same place in the word: first, next to last, and so on. In English stress is more variable than that, and the position of stress has shifted in numerous words in the last few centuries. (However, as we shall see in Chapter 8, there are great regularities in how polysyllabic words are stressed.)

Speakers of English differ in the pronunciation of specific words, and we notice this fact easily; *half*, *either*, *tomato* are commonly cited examples. What we probably fail to recognize is that the differences are almost entirely in vowels, scarcely at all in consonants. Chapter 5 explores the vowels in different varieties of the language.

Thus mutual intelligibility requires a lot of shared vocabulary in spite of some differences; common grammar (morphology and syntax), again in spite of differences; and a system of pronouncing – a **phonology** – in which the differences are noted only because of the great similarities taken for granted.

1.4 Plan of this book

Each chapter, after this one, begins with a section called *Looking ahead*, which briefly outlines the main points to be treated in the chapter. Each chapter ends with a section called *Looking back*, which, as you might expect, summarizes those points but attempts to do more – to show the importance of what has been treated, or to describe some problems in analyzing not taken up within the chapter, some differences of opinion among linguists about these matters, and the like. Readings in other books are suggested for those who want to extend their exploration of these topics.

If you are a native speaker of English, you may find that some of the descriptive statements and some of the illustrative utterances do not agree with what you say. This is inevitable and does not mean that you are 'wrong' or that the book is in error. There is a limit to the variation that can be dealt with in a single volume. While the book cannot deal in detail with every variety of the language, we hope to provide a basis for understanding what kinds of variation exist, which should help you to understand better how your speech fits into the overall pattern of English phonology.

A description of the sound structure of English or any language requires a theoretical viewpoint. That viewpoint influences, or even determines, how we approach the subject and anything we accomplish contributes to that viewpoint. As we elaborate in Chapter 3, our concern is not with English pronunciation alone but with the sound system – the phonology – and its relation to the semantics and grammar of English. Our larger aim in any linguistic investigation is to acquire a better understanding of what language is, how it works, and what common knowledge people possess that enables them to communicate with each other.

Suggestions for outside reading

Those who do not have a strong background in linguistics – and even those who have – would do well to become acquainted with one or both of the following books, which admirably expound in laymen's language the aims, findings, and current controversies in the science:

Pinker, Steven. 1994. *The Language Instinct: How the Mind Creates Language*. New York: William Morrow.
Wardhaugh, Ronald. 1993. *Investigating Language: Central Problems in Linguistics*. Oxford: Blackwell.

Two large volumes that contain a wealth of information about the English language – history, varieties, phonology, writing, vocabulary, grammar, forms of discourse, and more – are:

Crystal, David. 1995. *The Cambridge Encyclopedia of the English Language*. Cambridge: Cambridge University Press.
McArthur, Tom, ed. 1992. *The Oxford Companion to the English Language*. Oxford and New York: Oxford University Press.

Those who want to delve deeper into English dialectology should be familiar with:

Trudgill, Peter, and Hannah, Jean. 1994. *International English: a Guide to Varieties of Standard English*. 3rd edn. London: Edward Arnold.

Trudgill and Hannah deal with all aspects of English in native-speaker varieties. The phonology – or phonologies – of those varieties and also the 'New Englishes' is the topic of:

Wells, J.C. 1982. *Accents of English*. 3 vols. Cambridge: Cambridge University Press.

Other works on native and non-native varieties of English are the following:

Bailey, Richard W. and Görlach, Manfred (eds). 1982. *English as a World Language*. Ann Arbor: University of Michigan Press.

Hughes, A. and Trudgill, Peter. 1987. *English Accents and Dialects*. 2nd edn. London: Edward Arnold.
Kachru, Braj B. 1986. *The Alchemy of English*. Oxford: Pergamon.
Platt J.T., Weber, H., and Ho, M.L. 1984. *The New Englishes*. London: Routledge & Kegan Paul.

Note

The word 'accents' is often used to refer to dialect differences of pronunciation. In this book **accent** is a technical term used in quite a different sense; see Chapter 7.

Chapter 2

Speech

- **2.1 The nature of sound**   14
- **2.2 Speech**   16
- **2.3 Consonants**   18
- **2.4 Vowels**   26
- **2.5 Syllables and prosodic features**   29

LOOKING AHEAD

Essentially all the sounds that we hear are the result of vibrations in the air around us. In Section 2.1 we first consider some of the physical characteristics of such vibrations: why sounds differ in loudness and in pitch or tone, and how secondary vibration, resonance, is important.

For practical purposes we limit our study of speech to the sounds that are made when air is expelled from the lungs and is modified in various ways as it moves upward and out of the body. The vocal cords in the larynx provide the basic vibration in the air stream, which is further modified above the larynx in the vocal tract. There are two kinds of modification: the vocal tract can be shaped in different ways so that air vibrates in different patterns of resonance, or the air stream can be obstructed, wholly or partly, in different places. Obstruction and resonance can occur together. (See Section 2.2.)

Obstruent consonants are made – articulated – by obstructing the flow of air, partially or completely. Sonorant consonants are articulated with obstruction and resonance together. To describe different consonant sounds we name the articulator that obstructs and the place of articulation. (See Section 2.3.)

Vowel sounds result from different patterns of resonance, which depend on how the mouth is shaped by different positions of the tongue and different lip shapes. (See Section 2.4.)

Speech sounds cluster together in syllables. Syllables differ in intensity or loudness, in pitch or tone, and in duration. These prosodic features can be used to signal differences of meaning. (See Section 2.5.)

2.1 The nature of sound

Any sound that we hear is the result of air vibrating, which can be caused in two ways: either a force is applied to a body that can vibrate, as when we slam a door, and the vibration of this body is transmitted to the particles of air that surround it, making them vibrate in the same way; or air itself is moving – the natural movement that we call 'wind,' for instance – and is displaced by various obstacles in its path. When we strike the strings of a guitar, violin, harp, or piano, we create a kind of controlled vibration: the strings vary in length and tension so that each vibrates at a particular frequency. When we pump air into the pipes of an organ or blow into a flute, trombone, or clarinet, vibration of air particles is controlled by the size and shape of the pipe or tube.

The **frequency** of a vibration is the number of cycles – back-and-forth movements – that the vibrating body makes in a unit of time; usually the unit of measurement is 1 second. The **amplitude** of the vibration is the maximum distance that the vibrating body moves. If you pluck one string of a guitar or a harp in one small area, that part of the string moves a certain distance back and forth – its amplitude – a certain number of times per second – its frequency. Other parts of the string move different distances at different frequencies and the particles of air along both sides of the string repeat these amplitudes and frequencies, transmitting the same vibrations to other particles of air, and so on. Thus what seems to be a simple sound is actually due to a complex set of vibrations.

If you strike a chord on the guitar or harp – cause several strings to vibrate, each at its own frequency – the pattern of vibrations is of course even more complex. An important part of the sound is due to **resonance**, the secondary vibration of air particles in a resonator, or resonance chamber, the body of the guitar or the hollow structure to which harp strings are attached at the bottom. Similarly, the pipes of an organ are a set of resonance chambers of different sizes; a clarinet, a trombone, and other wind instruments are tubes that can be altered to form resonance chambers of different sizes. The size and shape of a resonance chamber determine the pattern of vibration of the air particles in it. The quantity of air in the resonator of a stringed instrument is fixed, while in the resonance chamber of a wind instrument the air is moving and so is subject to different forces. The force used in vibrating a stringed instrument or in propelling air into a wind instrument determines the intensity of a sound: the greater the force, the louder the sound. The length and tension of strings and the size and shape of resonance chambers determine the pitch or tone of the resultant sound; the greater the frequency of vibration, the higher the pitch.

2.2 Speech

Phonetics is the science that studies and describes speech sounds, that is, the sounds produced with the breath by all human beings as part of their language. This chapter introduces the general framework for description of all speech sounds but we concentrate mostly on what is important for describing English. The great majority of speech sounds in any language are produced with air expelled from the **lungs** (egressive lung air), so that the production of speech sounds is somewhat like playing a wind instrument. The lungs are surrounded by muscles – the diaphragm below and, on each side, muscles between the ribs (intercostal muscles). The muscles contract, reducing the volume of the lungs so that air is expelled (exhalation), and then they relax, increasing the volume so that air is drawn into the lungs from outside (inhalation).

The air expelled from the lungs passes up the **trachea** and enters the **larynx**, a structure of cartilage inside the neck. (See Figure 2.1.) Two bands of cartilage, called the vocal bands, or vocal folds, or **vocal cords**, stretch from the front to the back of the larynx. The vocal cords can be closed together to shut off the flow of air or opened and held with different degrees of tension; then they vibrate with different frequencies. If you open your mouth wide to say "Ah" and sing up and down the scale, you are changing the tension of the vocal cords and therefore the frequency of their vibration.

Just as the lungs provide the force – the flow of air – for speech, the vocal cords furnish the primary vibration. All speech sounds to be considered in this chapter are made by modifying the flow of air at the vocal cords or above the larynx in the **vocal tract**.

The space between the vocal cords is called the **glottis**. Closing and opening the vocal cords we make a sound called a **glottal stop**, for which the phonetic symbol is [ʔ], a question mark with a stroke drawn straight down and no dot. You probably make a glottal stop when you cough and when you say "Oh-oh" and also when, instead of saying "No," you make the vocal gesture that is written "Unh-unh." Instead of making a stop with the vocal cords, we can separate them slightly, and then the air passing through this narrow opening creates friction, a **glottal fricative** sound, symbolized with [h], the sound you make to begin the word *happy*, for example. (As you see, symbols for speech sounds, or **phones**, are enclosed in square brackets.)

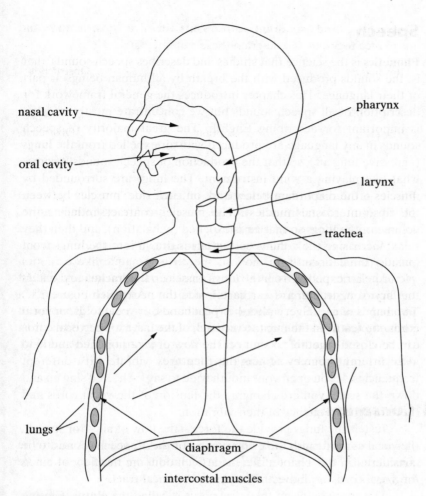

nasal cavity

oral cavity

pharynx

larynx

trachea

lungs

diaphragm

intercostal muscles

FIGURE 2.1 The vocal apparatus

Air moves from the larynx into the **pharynx** (the area behind the mouth) and then the **nasal cavity**, or the **oral cavity** (the mouth), or both together. These three areas make up the **vocal tract**, which can be shaped in various ways to create different resonance chambers. In the vocal tract also the air may be obstructed, wholly or partially, in different places. Speech sounds, then, may be the result of resonance or obstruction, or both together. **Vowel** sounds are the result of pure resonance, **obstruent consonants** are produced by complete or partial obstruction, and **sonorant consonants** involve obstruction and resonance together. To diagram these statements:

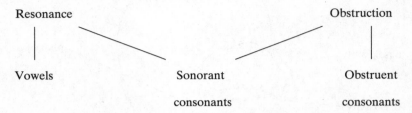

Resonance   Obstruction

Vowels   Sonorant   Obstruent

                              consonants   consonants

Phones produced with resonance are musical, due to regular patterns of vibration. Phones made without resonance are essentially noise, irregular vibration or no vibration.

When we speak, the vocal cords, tongue, lips, and velum (or soft palate) are constantly in motion; speech is dynamic like a motion picture. Each phone is like one frame in the film; at any instant the lips, tongue, etc. are in a certain position. Any such position is a **phonetic feature**. Every phone is produced by a unique grouping of phonetic features – the lips are open or closed, the tongue is touching the roof of the mouth or not, vocal cords are vibrating or not – and we describe any phone by naming these features.

2.3 Consonants

A speech sound made with obstruction of the air stream is said to be **articulated**. To describe different articulations we need to take note of these kinds of phonetic features:

(a) the manner of articulation;
(b) the articulator and place of articulation;
(c) voicing: whether the vocal cords are vibrating or not;
(d) the shape of the tongue and the lips.

Manner of articulation

As indicated in Section 2.2, consonants are of two sorts: obstruent consonants, made with obstruction and without resonance, and sono-rant consonants, in which there is obstruction and resonance.

Obstruent consonants include **plosives**, in which the obstruction is complete, and **fricatives**, in which the obstruction is partial. One plosive is [p], as in the middle of the word *copy* and at the end of the word *cup*. Say *copy* and note how your lips close and open again; say *cup* and note that your lips close and may or may not open again. One fricative is [f] as in the middle of *coffee* and at the end of *cuff*. Say these words and notice how your lower lip rests lightly on the edges of your upper front teeth for the articulation of [f]. The air stream moves through this narrow passage between lip and teeth, creating friction or turbulence. Compare *cuff* and *cup*. You can prolong the [f] as long as you have breath since the air is coming out between lip and teeth; you can't prolong the [p] because air is not escaping.

Sonorant consonants include **nasals** and **liquids**. The former are produced with occlusion in the mouth while air escapes through the nasal cavity; the latter are produced with air exiting from the mouth around the tongue when the tongue has a particular shape. One nasal is [m], as in the middle of *comic* and at the end of *come*. Compare *cup* and *come*. You end both words with the lips closed together, yet you can make [m] last as long as you have breath (just as you can hum with lips closed) whereas [p] cannot be prolonged. Air cannot escape from the mouth but – as the term 'nasal' indicates – it comes out of the nose for [m]. At the back of the mouth, between the pharynx and the nasal cavity is the **velum**, or soft palate. The velum is like a door: it opens and air enters the nasal cavity; it closes and entrance is impossible. For the plosive [p] the velum is closed as well as the lips; for [m] the velum is open and the lips closed. Figure 2.2 is a schematic drawing that shows the difference in manner of articulation between [p] (and [b]) and [m].

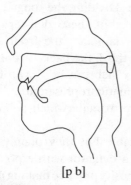
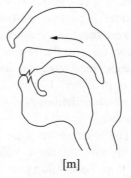

[p b]   [m]

FIGURE 2.2

Liquids are articulated with the tongue raised, partly impeding the flow of air, but the tongue is shaped in such a way that air flows around it, creating particular patterns of vibration. One liquid is [ɹ], as at the beginning of *red*. Note how your tongue is pulled back and bunched up toward the roof of your mouth, and there is a slight groove in the tip of your tongue.

Articulator and place of articulation

All plosives are articulated by stopping the air somewhere in the mouth, without other exit. All nasals require stopping the air in some part of the mouth while air is escaping through the nasal cavity. All fricatives involve 'squeezing' the air stream in some part of the vocal tract. All of these require an articulator, which moves, and a point of articulation which the articulator touches or comes close to. The articulators are the lower lip and different parts of the tongue, a muscular organ attached in back but otherwise very mobile. Muscles in the face and jaw assist in articulations.

Roughly speaking, the points of articulation lie along the upper edge of the vocal tract. From front to back these are: the **upper lip**; the upper front **teeth**; the alveolus, or **alveolar ridge**, the terrace-like structure behind the upper teeth; the **palate**, or 'hard palate,' the dome-like part of the mouth, above which is a bony structure separating mouth and nasal cavity; the **velum** or 'soft palate,' that part of the roof which has no bone above it; and, far back, the wall of the **pharynx**. Articulators lie along the lower edge of the vocal tract and include the **lower lip** – responsible for the articulation of [p f m], as we have seen – and parts of the tongue. Dividing the tongue into articulators is rather arbitrary, of course, but these divisions are customary: the tip, or **apex**; the blade, or **lamina** – the front third of the top surface; the **center** – the middle third; the back, or **dorsum** – the back third; and the root, or **radix**, which can be drawn back into the pharynx. Figure 2.3 is a schematic representation that shows which articulators can touch or approximate which points of articulation.

The nine terms may seem formidable but they plainly and accurately indicate the conjunction of an articulator with a point of articulation. To develop your phonetic virtuosity practice making nasal consonants at eight of these places of articulation. (We give the IPA

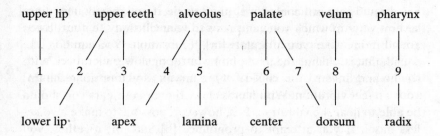

1 bilabial 2 labiodental 3 apicodental 4 apicoalveolar 5 laminoalveolar
6 centropalatal 7 dorsopalatal 8 dorsovelar 9 radicopharyngeal

FIGURE 2.3

symbols but learning them is not essential for doing the phonetic exercise.)

Bilabial [m]: In *comic* and *come*, for instance.

Labiodental [ɱ]: Put lower lip against the cutting edge of your upper front teeth and let air come out of the nose; you probably articulate this consonant in *emphasis* and *symphony*, for example.

Apicodental [n̪]: Tongue-tip against upper front teeth; possibly this is what you articulate in *tenth* or *in there*.

Apicoalveolar [n]: Tongue-tip against alveolar ridge; what you may articulate in *nice*, for example.

Laminoalveolar [n̟]: Front of tongue against alveolar ridge; very likely your articulation in *lunch* or *orange*.

Centropalatal [ɲ]: Center of tongue against the palate; the consonant that occurs in French *agneau* 'lamb' and Spanish *baño* 'bath.'

Dorsopalatal [ŋ]: Back of tongue against the 'hard' palate; you probably articulate this or something near it in the word *sing*.

Dorsovelar [ŋ]: Back of tongue against the 'soft' palate, or velum; your articulation in *song*, for example.

Voicing

Before discussing plosives and fricatives we need to consider another kind of phonetic feature. When we articulate a consonant, the vocal cords are vibrating or not vibrating; the articulation is either **voiced** or

voiceless. The nasal consonants just practiced are voiced. There are several ways in which you can prove to yourself that the vocal cords are vibrating when you articulate [m], for example. You can hum the sound, that is, change the tone of it by faster or slower vibration. With thumb and fingers on each side of the larynx as you prolong the [m] you can feel vibration. With hands clasped over your ears you should be able to hear the vibration. It is, however, possible to make a voiceless nasal. If you attempt to pronounce [h] and [m] together, you should produce a voiceless bilabial nasal.

In English and many languages fricatives and plosives exist in pairs that differ only in voicing. For instance, [p] as in *cup* and [b] as in *cub* are both bilabial plosives, the first voiceless and the second voiced. [f] as in *leaf* and [v] as in *leave* are, respectively, a voiceless labiodental fricative and a voiced labiodental fricative. In articulating plosives it is rather hard to apply the tests for voicing but with fricatives the tests work quite well. Feel the vibration as you articulate [v]; listen for the vibration; sing [v] up and down the scale. Then try to do these things with [f]. (See Figure 2.4.)

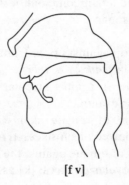

[f v]

FIGURE 2.4

Figure 2.5 shows symbols for the nasal consonants you have practiced and also symbols for plosives and fricatives articulated with the same articulators and points of articulation.

Referring to Figure 2.5, practice the following plosives and fricatives that can be found in English:

voiceless and voiced apicodental fricatives, [θ] as in *thin* and *breath*, [ð] as in *then* and *breathe* (also see Figure 2.6);

	Nasal	*Plosive*	*Fricative*
Bilabial	m	p b	ɸ β
Labiodental	ɱ		f v
Apicodental	n̪	t̪ d̪	θ ð
Apicoalveolar	n	t d	s z
Laminoalveolar	n̩		ʃ ʒ
Centropalatal	ɲ	c ɟ	ç ʝ
Dorsopalatal	ŋ̟	k̟ ɡ̟	x̟ ɣ̟
Dorsovelar	ɡ	k ɡ	x ɣ
Radicopharyngeal			ħ ʕ

FIGURE 2.5

[θ ð]

FIGURE 2.6

voiceless and voiced apicoalveolar plosives, [t] as in *bat* and [d] as in
    bad (Figure 2.7);
voiceless and voiced dorsovelar plosives, [k] as in *tack* and [ɡ] as in
    tag (Figure 2.8).

Some other plosives and fricatives, which do not occur in English, are
    these:

voiceless bilabial fricative [ɸ] as in Japanese *Fuji*;
voiced bilabial fricative [β] in the middle of Spanish *Cuba*;
voiceless dorsovelar fricative [x] at the end of German *Bach* or the
    beginning of Russian *xorošo* 'thanks';
voiceless radicopharyngeal fricative [ħ] at the beginning of Arabic
    ħammaam 'bath';

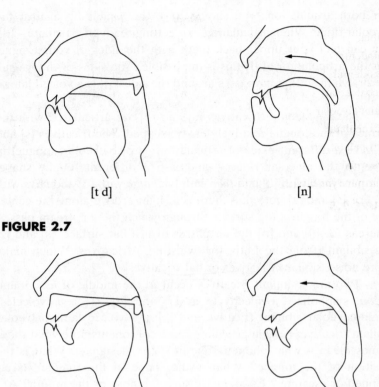

[t d]   [n]

FIGURE 2.7

[k g]   [ŋ]

FIGURE 2.8

voiced radicopharyngeal fricative [ʕ] at the beginning of Arabic *ʕamm* 'uncle.'

Tongue shape

For some consonant articulations the shape of the tongue is an important phonetic feature. We have already noted that the liquid [ɹ] is made with the tongue drawn back and bunched up and there is a slight groove in the tip. We describe this articulation by saying that [ɹ] is a voiced retroflex liquid. Another liquid is [l] as in *lie* and *rely*. Compare what you do in pronouncing the [d] of *die* and the [l] of *lie*.

For both articulations you should have the tongue-tip against the alveolar ridge. When articulating – or getting ready to articulate – [d], you can feel your upper back teeth with the sides of your tongue. For the articulation of [l] this is impossible. The sides of the tongue are drawn in so that air passes around the sides: [l] is a voiced lateral liquid.

The apicodental fricatives [θ] and [ð] are articulated with the surface of the tongue relatively flat, unshaped. The fricatives [s and [z] have a different place of articulation – apicoalveolar: tongue-tip close to the alveolar ridge – and also a different tongue shape. Compare *faith* with [θ] and *face* with [s], *bathe* with [ð] and *bays* with [z]. For [s] and [z] note that there is a slight groove along the center line of the tongue's top surface through which the air stream passes, whereas for [θ] and [ð] the air passes over a flat surface. [s] and [z] are sibilant (from the Latin for 'whistling') fricatives. Which make more noise, sibilant fricatives or flat fricatives?

Two more sibilant fricatives occur in the middle of *fission* and *vision*, symbolized respectively as [ʃ] and [ʒ]. [ʃ] is a voiceless laminoalveolar sibilant fricative and [ʒ] is a voiced laminoalveolar sibilant fricative. As you articulate these consonants note what those names mean – what phonetic features they designate. What is the position of the tongue? What is the shape of the tongue? Is air stopped or escaping? Escaping through the nose or the mouth? Are the vocal cords vibrating or not? These questions, of course, are relevant for describing any consonant articulation.

PRACTICE 2.1

1 Without looking back, fill out the chart below to indicate what articulator and what point of articulation are named by each term. The first is filled in as an example.

	Articulator	*Point of articulation*
labiodental	lower lip	upper teeth
dorsovelar		
laminoalveolar		
centropalatal		
apicodental		

> 2 Which of the following words *end* with a nasal? Which ones *begin* with a fricative? (Sounds, not letters.)
>
> doom thumb sand vote bang shun look

2.4 Vowels

The nature – or **quality** – of any vowel sound depends on the shape of the area in which particles of air vibrate. When you say "Ah," the tongue is flat and the area from the lips back to the wall of the pharynx is a single cavity. If the tongue is raised and/or moved forward, it divides this area into two cavities: an anterior area from the tongue to the roof of the mouth and forward to the lips; and a posterior area from the tongue back to the pharyngeal wall. If the lips are pushed outward, the anterior area is enlarged somewhat. Thus the quality of a vowel sound depends on (1) what part of the tongue is raised, if any, (2) how high it is raised, and (3) whether the lips are rounded and therefore pushed forward slightly.

To describe a specific vowel sound, we tell the position of the tongue in the mouth, and to do this with any degree of accuracy, we need to agree on certain conventions. We draw imaginary lines that divide the oral cavity into areas, or we imagine points of reference at equal distances from one another in the mouth, or we do both of these things. Just as we locate any place in the world by using imaginary lines that indicate latitude and longitude, to describe vowels we use reference points in the mouth. The English phonetician Daniel Jones proposed a series of **cardinal vowels**, taking into account the most extreme positions in which vowels can be produced – the highest and lowest possible positions and the farthest forward and farthest back. Figure 2.9 shows the first eight of these cardinal vowels.

Cardinal Vowel 1, [i], is produced with the lips stretched and the front of the tongue in the highest and most forward position possible. If the tongue were any higher, there would be friction resulting from the flow of air between tongue and palate. Cardinal Vowel 4, [a], is produced with the lips stretched and the tongue front in the lowest and most forward position possible. Dividing the imaginary line between 1 and 4 into three equal parts, we designate two other cardinal vowels, 2, [e], and 3, [ɛ]. The line is at an angle because that is the nature of

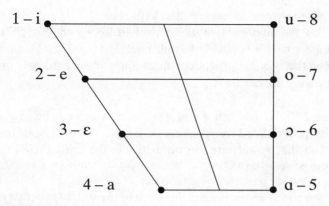

FIGURE 2.9

the human mouth; the tongue-front – the lamina – can move farther forward at the top of the mouth than at the bottom.

Cardinal Vowel 5 [ɑ] is produced with the tongue flat, the lowest, farthest back position the tongue can have in the mouth. Cardinal Vowel 8 [u] is made with lips rounded and the dorsum in the highest and farthest back position possible. We divide the line from 5 to 8 into three equal parts and thus we designate Cardinal Vowels 6 [ɔ] and 7 [o].

Vowels 1, 2, 3, and 4 are unrounded (lips stretched to some extent), 5 is unrounded but lips are not stretched, and 6, 7, and 8 are rounded. We should note that Vowel 8 is not really as high as Vowel 1; the shape of the mouth prohibits our raising the tongue as high in back as in front; consequently the distance between 5, 6, 7, and 8 is not as great as the distance between 1, 2, 3, and 4.

It is dangerous to equate the cardinal vowels with vowels in English words because speakers of English differ considerably in the vowels they pronounce (though consonants are nearly identical in all dialects of English). Chapter 5 is a detailed treatment of these dialect differences. The following comparisons may help you to recognize these eight cardinal vowels:

[i] is like the vowel in *tree, treat*, kept short.
[e] is like the first part of the vowel in *day, date*.
[ε] is the vowel in *step*.
[a] may be the first part of the vowel in *tie, tide*.
[ɑ] is what the doctor asks you to say when she wants to look into your throat – perhaps your vowel in *spa, father*.

[ɔ] may be the vowel in *law*, *caught*, kept short.

[o] may be the first part of the vowel in *go*, *goat*, though the cardinal vowel is probably farther back.

[u] may be the vowel of *true*, kept short, though the cardinal vowel is probably farther back.

Figure 2.10 has nine other vowel symbols, which can be equated with vowels pronounced by speakers of English – keeping in mind again the fact that vowels are not phonetically the same throughout the English-speaking world.

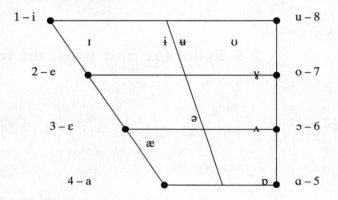

FIGURE 2.10

[ɪ] is possibly your vowel in *chick* or *fish*.

[ɨ] is a similar vowel made with the center of the tongue raised.

[ʊ] is, at least for many speakers, the vowel of *foot*.

[ʉ] is similar but made with the center of the tongue.

[æ] may be your vowel of *bat*.

[ə] called schwa, is the first and last vowel of *arena*.

[ɣ] has the tongue position of [o] but with lips unrounded.

[ʌ] has the tongue position of [ɔ] but with lips unrounded.

[ɒ] has the tongue position of [ɑ] but with lips slightly rounded.

The words below are arranged in **minimal pairs**. They differ only in the vowel. Carefully examine your own pronunciation and decide, for each pair, which word has the vowel made with the tongue higher in the mouth.

bit, bet   buck, book   fat, fate
low, law   seat, sit   Luke, look

2.5 Syllables and prosodic features

When we produce a stream of speech, lips, tongue, vocal cords and velum are in constant motion as we have noted (Section 2.2), and yet we perceive that stream of speech as a sequence of phones. These phones are organized into syllables, and each syllable has a peak, or nucleus, which is usually a vowel, with consonants clustered around the vowel. Syllables differ from one another in three possible ways:

Duration. Some syllables are longer than others; the speaker prolongs the peaks or other parts of some syllables in contrast to other syllables.
Stress. Some syllables are produced with greater intensity – greater force with which air is expelled from the lungs, which makes a difference of loudness.
Tone, or pitch. Syllables may be produced with the vocal cords vibrating relatively fast (high pitch) or slow (low pitch) or increasing in rate of vibration (rising pitch) or slowing down the rate of vibration (falling pitch). There can be different degrees of pitch height in different syllables and different combinations of falling and rising within a single syllable.

How these kinds of prosodic features are used depends on what language we are dealing with. In German *Staat* 'state' and *Stadt* 'city' the principal difference is that the vowel of the first word is longer than that of the second word; vowel length is used to differentiate words. In English some vowels are longer than others but there are no two vowels that differ only in length. A speaker can prolong a vowel in order to be more emphatic, more 'expressive,' but duration is not used to distinguish one word from another.

Some languages use stress functionally – to make distinctions between words, as with English ínsult (noun) versus insúlt (verb). In other languages the stressed syllable of a word is always the first syllable, or the last syllable, or the penultimate syllable – that is, always in the same place so that words cannot be differentiated by stress.

All languages use pitch differences for intonation, the melodies that go with whole utterances. In English, for example, any utterance spoken with a falling pitch at the end – "Yes" or "Nineteen" or "Potatoes are cheaper now" – will be interpreted as a statement and the same spoken with rising pitch will be taken as a question, a request for clarification. Some languages, called tone languages, have a system of pitch differences to distinguish words from one another. A much-used illustration is the four tones of Mandarin Chinese.

> mā (high level) 'mother'
> má (high rising) 'hemp'
> mǎ (falling–rising) 'horse'
> mà (high falling) 'to scold'

Physically, duration, stress, and pitch are three different kinds of prosodic features, but in English it often happens that a syllable with changing pitch is also the syllable with greatest stress and perhaps the longest syllable as well. At any rate, these prosodic features are just as important as other phonetic features and they must receive as much attention as vowels and consonants in a description of spoken English.

LOOKING BACK

Sounds that we hear are due to the vibration of some body in the air around us. Vibration results either because a moving body displaces particles of air or because air in motion is displaced or channeled into some container. Sounds produced either way differ from one another in loudness, which is due to differences of force, and/or in pitch, which is due to the frequency with which particles of air move back and forth. Sounds may also differ in duration.

The vibrations in any sound are complex, some of them due to secondary vibrations called resonance. Especially notable are secondary vibrations within a (partially) closed space, a resonance chamber. The size and shape of the resonance chamber determine the quality of the resultant sound.

Speech sounds are mostly made with egressive lung air. Air moves from the lungs up the trachea and enters a box of cartilage called the larynx. In the larynx the vocal cords, when tense and close together, vibrate in response to the outgoing air. Their degree of tension determines the frequency of vibration. This basic vibration is further modified in the vocal tract, which can be shaped in various ways, providing different resonances. In the vocal tract also the air may be obstructed, wholly or partially, in different places. Speech sounds, then, may be the result of resonance, or obstruction, or both together. While modifications are taking place in the vocal tract – the pharynx, nasal cavity, and oral cavity – the vocal cords vibrate or remain motionless, producing, respectively, voiced or voiceless sounds. (Articulations may be accompanied by vocal cord vibration or not, resulting, respectively, in voiced or voiceless speech sounds.)

Vowels are speech sounds produced with resonance, obstruent consonants are produced – articulated – by obstructing the flow of air, and sonorant consonants involve both obstruction and resonance. Obstruent consonants include plosives, in which the obstruction is complete, and fricatives, in which the obstruction is partial. Sonorant consonants include nasals and liquids. The former are produced with occlusion in the mouth while air escapes through the nasal cavity; the latter are produced with air exiting from the mouth around the tongue when the tongue has a particular shape.

An articulation is the action of some articulator in conjunction with a place of articulation. Articulators are the lower lip and different parts of the tongue. Places of articulation are the upper lip, different parts of the roof of the mouth, and the wall of the pharynx.

The nature of vowels – pure resonance – depends on the size of two dimensions in the mouth: the distance between the highest part of the tongue and the lips; and the distance between the body of the tongue and the pharyngeal wall. The rounding and/or protrusion of the lips creates another dimension that contributes to the quality of a vowel. To describe different vowel sounds, then, we take into account tongue height, tongue advancement, and whether the lips are rounded or not. Phoneticians have long used a set of cardinal vowels

– four equidistant points from highest possible vowel to lowest possible vowel in front and in back, with further distinctions between unrounded and rounded vowels and vowels at intermediate points.

Besides production of vowel and consonant sounds phonetics also describes prosodic features of speech. The most important of these is pitch, acoustic differences due to different frequencies with which the vocal cords vibrate. Any voiced sound can be produced at a relatively high or relatively low pitch, or with pitch changing from higher to lower or vice versa.

Suggested readings

A more extensive treatment of the physiology of speech production is Ladefoged (1993: Chapter 1). A still more detailed description is Clark and Yallop (1995: Chapter 2).

Note

Anyone who consults different texts on phonetics will find some differences in terminology and ways of classifying. The terms used here for divisions of the tongue surface follow Ladefoged (1993). The use of compound terms for designating articulations, naming both the articulator and the point of articulation – apicodental, lamino-alveolar, etc. – originated with Hockett (1955). Unfortunately, most phoneticians have continued to use a set of traditional names, which sometimes designate articulator and place articulation ('labiodental'), sometimes just the place of articulation ('palatal,' 'velar').

Chapter 3

The structure of language

- **3.1 Units of language**   34
- **3.2 Knowing one's native language** 37
- **3.3 Phonemes**   39

LOOKING AHEAD

Speaking to other people and understanding what they say is much more than producing and hearing speech sounds. Section 3.1 discusses the organization of language and the ways that meanings are communicated. People who can communicate in a language must have certain shared knowledge and we need to specify just what this common knowledge is. (See Section 3.2.)

In speaking our language we produce a multitude of different speech sounds – phones – far more than we are aware of until we begin to study phonetics. These phones are organized into a much smaller number of **phonemes**, the units in the sound system of the language. We are well aware of phonemes in our language because they make possible differences of meaning. Section 3.3 deals at some length with the difference between phones and phonemes, between phonetics and phonology.

3.1 Units of language

'Speaking' includes a great variety of activities: a single shout for help, an exchange of greetings, a conversation, a prayer recited aloud, a formal lecture, a three-act play, and much more. We use the term spoken **discourse** for any act of speech that takes place in a given place and within a given period of time, whether delivered by telephone, radio, television, or face to face. Similarly, there are many forms of written discourse: a business report, a newspaper article, a love letter, and a short story, among others. People talk to themselves sometimes, to animal pets, and even to inanimate objects, but our interest in speech is naturally confined to discourse in which humans interact with one another – in which there is a speaker and one or more hearers, possibly taking turns in speaking.

A spoken discourse consists of at least one **utterance**, which is defined as a stretch of speech produced by a single speaker, with silence – no matter how brief – before and after on the part of that speaker. A written discourse consists of at least one sentence, and our educational systems and editorial offices have established fairly strict standards of what a sentence should be. An utterance of spoken discourse may be like a written or printed sentence ("It's quite warm today," for instance), and lectures and sermons which are carefully prepared in advance may consist entirely of such utterances, but spoken discourse is different from written. Many utterances are fragmentary ("Can't") or jumbled ("The manager will maybe – er, I mean – may want more information"). Discourse markers are frequent ("Well . . . ," "And then . . . ," "As a matter of fact, . . . "). It is true of both spoken utterances and written sentences that they can sometimes be interpreted only with respect to previous parts of the discourse ("Yes, they did," for instance) but it is more true of spoken discourse. Later in this book, especially in Chapter 10, we discuss the relation of utterances to the total discourse, but for now let's deal only with utterances that are like sentences and can be considered in isolation.

Any utterance has a meaning: the speaker intends to convey a message and, if communication is successful, the hearer's interpretation matches the speaker's intention. Some of the hearer's interpretation may be derived from the utterance situation, perhaps from knowledge of the speaker, from the speaker's looks and gestures, and from the fact that they belong to the same culture. These sources of information are important – when a speaker of English makes a remark about the weather, for instance, the speaker's real intention may be to initiate a conversation and the hearer will probably recognize this. However, we are concerned here with linguistic meanings, those that are *conveyed in* an utterance itself.

Linguistic meanings are of two kinds. Most obviously, there are **lexical** meanings: we use nouns like *map* and *medicine* to refer to various entities, even imaginary or hypothetical ones, and verbs and adjectives such as *buy*, *bring*, *new*, *excellent* to say something about entities. Lexical meanings are expressed in **words**. A single word may contain more than one unit of meaning, called a **morpheme**. The words *armchair*, *unhappy*, and *guitarist* contain two morphemes each: *arm*, *chair*, *un-*, *happy*, *guitar*, *-ist*. The prefix *un-* and the suffix *-ist* are bound morphemes: they do not occur by themselves. *Arm*, *chair*, *happy*, and *guitar* are free morphemes; each of them has the status of a word without being attached to anything. (There is more about morphemes and word-structure in Chapter 8.)

There are **grammatical** meanings, conveyed in various ways. Some meanings are expressed in the order of words. To use a hackneyed example, "The dog bit a man" and "The man bit a dog" have the same words but different meanings, and "The a man dog bit" has no meaning. Grammatical meanings are also expressed in endings like the *-s* of *maps* and the *-ed* of *looked*, and in function words like *the, of, not, who* which do not name entities or make predications about entities but are indispensable for communicating. If we insert the word *not* into the utterance "David is looking at the map," we don't add a meaning; we change the meaning of the whole utterance: "David is not looking at the map." If we replace *David* with *Who*, we create a different sort of utterance: "Who is looking at the map?" Finally, meanings are conveyed by **prosody**, different uses of emphasis and melody due to variations in the force with which air is expelled from the lungs and in the frequency of vocal cord vibration. "This map is new" is a statement if spoken with a falling tone, a question if the tone rises; "I WON'T attend the meeting" says something different from "I won't attend the MEETING." (Chapters 10 and 11 have much more about these prosodic matters.)

If two people can communicate through language, then they must have shared knowledge. They have to have a vocabulary in common, attaching fairly much the same meanings to most of the words they use and attaching pronunciations to those words which are enough alike that each recognizes (almost instantly) what the other intends. They must have the same grammatical knowledge, producing and interpreting constructions in the same way, though there may be nuances of difference. And they use roughly the same prosodic system even if they sometimes note differences in how they use it.

People who speak different dialects have some different pronunciations and they attach different meanings to some words or express certain meanings with different words. These differences can lead to misunderstandings, but they are not big enough to prevent communication. Dialects of a language are **mutually intelligible**.

When we listen to someone talking, our ears take in a sequence of sounds but our brain apparently works differently. We do not grasp the meaning of an utterance by processing one sound after another nor even one word after another. We organize what we hear into phrases, groups of words, and these presumably correspond to phrases that the speaker is producing. In speech we call such a phrase a **tone unit**. Speakers do not necessarily pause between tone units, but they are more likely to pause between, rather than within, tone units. For example, an utterance like the following one might be spoken with pauses in at least one of the places marked with a vertical line (|):

I'll be glad to help you | as soon as I'm free | but just now | I'm afraid I can't manage any more than what I'm doing.

Every tone unit contains at least one **syllable**. The utterance "Help!" is one utterance, one tone unit, one word, and one syllable. Many words consist of more than one syllable, of course, and most tone units contain more than one word.

A syllable consists of at least one segment and usually, of course, more than one. Thus discourse, utterance, tone unit, syllable, and segment are the units to be recognized for describing speech.

3.2 Knowing one's native language

To describe a language is, at least from one point of view, to account for the knowledge that speakers of that language have which enables them to communicate with others who share that knowledge. Knowledge of a language must include a vocabulary and ways to use it. Nobody knows all the words in a large dictionary but we all have a vocabulary big enough to express what we want to express and, though vocabulary keeps growing, we are suitably equipped to understand what we need to understand in our daily activities. As speakers we have to know how to produce the sounds that express units of meaning and how to arrange these in meaningful utterances. As listeners we have to be able to recognize the meanings that are signaled in the sounds and arrangements that others produce. Speakers of a language know part of the vocabulary or lexicon of the language and they know the phonology and grammar that express the vocabulary. They know meanings expressed in words and meanings expressed in utterances (*Dog bites man, Man bites dog*, etc.).

When we say that speakers of a language know the phonology of their language, we mean that they can accurately produce the sequences of sounds that signal different meanings and that they can recognize the sequences of sounds produced by other speakers and can connect these sequences to the meanings intended by those speakers. But ordinary speakers do not 'know' in the sense that they can describe the complex manipulations of their vocal organs in pronouncing. Any native speaker of English can pronounce and recognize *beat*, *bit*, *meat*, and *meek*, but the ability to explain how *bit* differs from *beat*, and *beat* from *meat* and *meat* from *meek*, is not part of native-speaker knowledge. This is the sort of thing one learns from a study of phonetics.

Ordinary speakers of a language do not know all about the production of speech sounds in their language, but they know – unconsciously – the functional units of sound in their language. Speakers of English know if two English words are the same or different; they know, for instance, that *sin* and *thin* are different and so are *cheap* and *sheep*, and *sheep* and *ship*, though these slight differences of sound may not be apparent to speakers of other languages. Sounds that are only slightly different constitute different **phonemes** because they are used to distinguish English words of different meanings. Phonemes are units of sound which combine in various possible ways (but not all possible ways) to express meaningful units such as words. Speakers of a language need not know the word 'phoneme' but they are aware of the phonemes of that language. They can identify any phoneme by matching it with some phoneme in another word or in the same word. For example,

1   The words *pie* and *spy* both contain bilabial plosives. Are they the same?
2   Do the words *dip* and *dim* have the same vowel?
3   Is the consonant at the beginning of *leaf* the same as the consonant at the end of *feel*?

These are 'trick' questions because the answers depend on how we interpret 'the same.' The *p*-sounds in *pie* and *spy* are different phonetically because the first is aspirated and the second is not, but in English this physical difference is not significant. The two phones are members of the same English phoneme. In that sense they are 'the same.' Similarly, as we explore in Section 3.3, the vowels of *dip* and *dim* are phonetically different but belong to the same English phoneme, and the lateral consonants in *leaf* and *feel* involve different articulations – at least for some speakers – but the difference does not matter *in English*. Speakers of a language do not know the phonetics of their languages – the details of speech production – but they know the phonology; they know when different sounds function as different, making possible differences of meaning like *thin* and *sin*, and they do not recognize different speech sounds that do not function differently in their language like the two plosives in *paper*.

Similarly, a speaker knows how to combine words into complex sentences and to grasp the meanings of complex structures that other speakers produce. Any adolescent or adult speaker can produce and can understand a sentence like *We shouldn't expect whoever took these things to be likely to want to return them*, but few speakers would be able to explain the syntax of it.

3.3 Phonemes

One part of Chapter 2 called attention to several nasal phones that you could recognize fairly easily:

[m]   a bilabial nasal in *come* or *rum*;
[ɱ]   a labiodental nasal that you may pronounce in *emphasis*;
[n̪]   an apicodental nasal in *tenth* or in *there*;
[n]   an apicoalveolar nasal in *run*;
[n̻]   a laminoalveolar nasal in *lunch*;
[ɲ]   a dorsopalatal nasal in *sing*;
[ŋ]   a dorsovelar nasal in *sung* or *rung*.

That makes seven. Does English have seven different nasal consonants? That depends on how we define 'nasal consonant.' There are seven nasal phones but they are not in contrast with one another. English has three nasal **phonemes**, demonstrated in the words *rum*, *run*, *rung* (or *sum*, *sun*, *sung* or *Kim*, *kin*, *king*). A phone is a single speech sound (without regard for what language it may belong to). A phoneme is a unit of sound in a particular language. A phoneme has different pronunciations. These different pronunciations are phones that have some phonetic feature(s) in common but also differ in some phonetic feature(s).

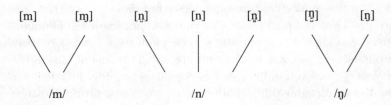

Note the use of virgules, or slant lines, to enclose the symbol for a phoneme, as distinct from square brackets around the symbol for a phone.

The English phoneme /m/ is articulated with the lower lip. It is articulated against the upper teeth – the phone [ɱ] – before /f/ as in *emphasis* or *symphony*. It is articulated with the two lips together – the phone [m] – in all other positions: *man, coma, number, rum*, etc.

The English phoneme /n/ is an apical or laminal nasal. It is apicodental [n̪] before /θ/ or /ð/ (as in *tenth, in there*); it is lamino-alveolar [n̺] before /č/ or /ǰ/ (as in *lunch* and *lunge*); it is apicoalveolar [n] elsewhere, as in *noon, candy, many, run*.

The English phoneme /ŋ/ is a dorsal nasal. It is dorsopalatal after front vowels [ŋ̟], as in *sing, sang* and dorsovelar after back vowels [ŋ], as in *song, sung*.

A phoneme, then, is a class of phones, called its **allophones**. The allophones do not contrast with one another: one occurs in one environment or group of environments, another somewhere else, another in other environments. Different phonemes, however, do contrast with one another; that is what makes *rum* different from *run* and *rung*, for instance. Any speaker of English, without ever thinking about articulation, is aware of these differences but is not aware that /n/ is different in *ten* and *tenth* nor /ŋ/ in *sing* and *song*. A speaker knows the phonology of the language, in a sense, just by being a speaker but does not know the phonetics without studying it. To summarize:

English nasal phonemes	Allophones
/m/ labial	[ɱ] labiodental before /f/
	[m] bilabial elsewhere
/n/ apical or laminal	[n̪] apicodental before /θ, ð/
	[n̺] laminoalveolar before /č, ǰ/
	[n] apicoalveolar elsewhere
/ŋ/ dorsal	[ŋ̟] after front vowels
	[ŋ] after back vowels

(We consider a different kind of analysis below.)

Now, let's turn from discussion of nasal consonants to nasalized vowels. Compare the words *dip* and *dim* and do a little experiment: start to say *dip* but don't close your lips at the end – don't pronounce a [p]. Start to say *dim* but don't close your lips – don't pronounce an [m]. Repeat the experiment with *hope* and *home*. You should observe that, when you intend to pronounce an [m], you produce a nasalized vowel and, when you intend to pronounce an non-nasal consonant like [p], there is no nasality in the vowel. If you are a native speaker of English, you probably had not been aware of this difference before reading the chapter – and that is as it should be; you had no reason to be aware. Nasalized [ĩ] and non-nasalized [ɪ], nasalized [õᵘ] and non-nasalized [oᵘ] are phonetically different – the physical facts are different – but in English the difference is not significant. Nasalized vowels occur before nasal consonants – *seem*, *dim*, *fan*, *long*, *home*, *don't*, etc. – and non-nasalized vowels occur where there is no nasal consonant following, as in *see*, *dip*, *fat*, *log*, *hope*, and so on.

If you learn to speak Portuguese or French, among other languages, you need to master the skill of producing nasalized vowels without a nasal consonant following. In Portuguese the word that means 'wool' is *lã* (nasalized vowel) and a word for 'there' is *lá* (non-nasalized). French *bas* 'stocking' is [ba] and *banc* 'bench' is [bã].

In the first years of life all humans have the same capacity for making speech sounds, but as we acquire the language spoken all around us we learn to use speech sounds according to the patterns of that language. Different languages have different patterns. Children who grow up speaking Portuguese or French learn to distinguish between certain pairs of vowels that differ only in nasality; children who grow up speaking English (among other languages) do not. We might say, instead, that English-speaking children learn a sort of automatic 'rule': if a vowel occurs before a nasal consonant, nasalize it. Obviously you didn't learn this in a conscious way, but then not all knowledge is conscious – we are not entirely aware of all we know.

As was pointed out in Chapter 2, phonetics is the science which studies and describes speech sounds as sounds, without regard for what function they have in any particular language. Phonetically, [a], [ã], [oᵘ], and [õᵘ] are all different sounds. **Phonology** is the account of how speech sounds function in a particular language or particular languages. In English, [oᵘ] and [õᵘ] function as a single unit called a phoneme. One of them occurs in one kind of environment, before nasal consonants, and the other occurs in all other kinds of environments. Therefore they are not in contrast with each other, cannot make a difference of meaning; there cannot be two English words such that one is pronounced [ho^u] and the other is pronounced [hõ^u]. There is an English phoneme /ou/ which has two pronunciations, or **allophones**, [o^u] and [õ^u]. Similarly, *bin* and *bid* have different allophones of a phoneme /ɪ/; *man* and *mad* have different allophones of a phoneme /æ/; *come* and *cub* have different allophones of a phoneme /ʌ/. On the other hand, Portuguese has two different phonemes /a/ and /ã/, and French has two phonemes /a/ and /ã/.

A phoneme, then, is an abstract unit that has more than one pronunciation – more than one realization in speech. In fact, it is easy to learn to recognize a number of realizations for almost any phoneme. The words *deem* and *doom* have the same initial phoneme, /d/, but in the first word that phoneme is articulated with the lips spread and in the second word with the lips rounded. The same is true, of course, for the phoneme /t/ in *team* and *tomb* and for the phoneme /n/ in *niece* and *noose*. These phonetic features, lip-spreading versus lip-rounding, are due to the fact that we, as speakers, anticipate the shape of the lips for the following vowels, just as nasality in the vowel of *home* is due to anticipation of the following consonant.

Comparing *geese* with *goose* and *keep* with *coop* leads to the same observation: the initial consonants of *geese* and *keep* are realized with lips spread, the initial consonants of *goose* and *coop* with lips rounded. And there is more: when you pronounce *geese* and *keep*, you can feel your tongue touching your palate for the initial consonant; when you pronounce the initial consonant of *gauze* and *caught*, the tongue makes its closure farther back, against the velum. The phoneme /g/ has two quite different allophones in *geese*, *goose*, and so of course does the phoneme /k/ in *keep*, *caught*.

Lip shape is not distinctive for the phonemes /d t n g k/; palatal versus velar closure is not distinctive for /g/ and /k/. But /d t n/ are always articulated with the tongue-tip and /g k/ are always articulated with the tongue-back. /d t g k/ are always plosives, made by completely stopping the flow of air; /n/ is always a nasal, articulated with stoppage of air in the mouth while air goes out of the nose. /t k/ are voiceless while /n d g/ are voiced. Each phoneme is defined by a set of distinctive features, the features which make it different from every other phoneme.

/n/   voiced apical nasal;
/d/   voiced apical plosive;
/t/   voiceless apical plosive;
/g/   voiced dorsal plosive;
/k/   voiceless dorsal plosive.

The distinctive features of a phoneme are present in all its allophones; the non-distinctive, or redundant, features are present in some allophones but not all. The difference between plosive and nasal makes /d/ distinct from /n/ so that *due* and *new* can have different meanings; the contrast of apical and dorsal makes /d/ distinct from /g/, making possible a distinction between *bad* and *bag*; the contrast of voiced and voiceless which keeps /d/ and /t/ apart enables English speakers to assign different meanings to *die* and *tie*.

The examples presented so far involve a kind of assimilation: consonants are articulated with lips spread before unrounded vowels and with lips rounded before rounded vowels; dorsal consonants are articulated more forward before front vowels and more back before back vowels; vowels have nasality before nasal consonants. All of this seems 'natural.' Let's consider another phoneme variation. The phoneme /l/ occurs initially in *lean*, *let*, *lace* and at the end of *kneel*, *tell*, *sail*. Compare the articulations. Initially the phoneme is a so-called 'clear' /l/; the front of the tongue is high, with the tip touching the alveolar ridge; the back of the tongue is down; and the sides are drawn in so that air escapes around the tongue. (As noted on pp. 24–5, if you compare /d/ and /l/ as in *die* and *lie*, you will find that the tongue-tip is in the same place for both; in pronouncing /d/ you can feel your back teeth with the sides of the tongue, something quite impossible when pronouncing /l/.) In final positions, at least for many speakers, /l/ is 'dark,' [ɫ]; the dorsum is high in the back of the mouth, the center is low, the front may be raised or not, and the tongue sides are drawn in. These two allophones, clear and dark, sound quite different, but they are not different because of the influence of following or preceding phonemes. It is simply a fact that English has an apical articulation for /l/ before vowels and a different articulation after vowels. With a little practice you can reverse these – say *tell* with a clear /l/ and *let* with a dark one. In both articulations the tongue-sides are curled in; this, of course, is the distinctive feature, laterality. No other English phoneme is lateral.

Let's consider another kind of variation. The phoneme /p/ occurs in the words *pie* and *spy* and twice in the word *paper*. Is it pronounced the same way in all four of these occurrences? Take a small strip of paper, hold it loosely in front of your mouth, and say the three words aloud. The paper should flutter for the first sound of *pie* and *paper*; it should not flutter for the stop in *spy* and perhaps not for the second stop in *paper*. The initial /p/ is aspirated in *pie*, *paper*, and the other two instances of the phoneme /p/ are unaspirated. When a plosive occurs in initial position, the air pressure is built up behind the articulator and place of articulation – in this case, behind the lips – and the vocal cords are slightly apart and motionless. When the lips open, air passes between the vocal cords, creating friction, a sound like [h]. The phonetic symbol for a voiceless bilabial stop with aspiration is [p^h]. After /s/ or a stressed vowel the air pressure behind the closed lips is not so great and aspiration does not occur. The phonetic symbol for an unaspirated voiceless bilabial stop is just [p]. [p^h] and [p] are allophones of the English phoneme /p/.

FLUENCY PRACTICE 3.1

Pronounce an aspirated [p^h] in *spy*. Say *pie* with an unaspirated [p]. Practice saying *paper* with [p^h] in both positions, then with [p] in both positions, then with [p] initially and [p^h] in the second position – the opposite of what is the norm for English.

Do the fluttering paper experiment with these sets of words:

tie sty tatter   kind sky khaki

You should find that the English phoneme /t/ has aspirated [t^h] and unaspirated [t] allophones, and the English phoneme /k/ likewise has aspirated [k^h] and unaspirated [k] allophones, and the occurrence of these allophones is exactly parallel to the aspirated and unaspirated allophones of the phoneme /p/.

A phonetic description of speech is a statement of physical facts; it tells what phones – speech sounds – are produced and in what order. A phonetic transcription, then, contains a symbol for each phone. Phonetic transcription of the English words *pin*, *spin*, *spit* and *bit* would be like this:

[pʰĩn] [spĩn] [spɪt] [bɪt]

A phonological (or phonemic) description of speech (in a particular language) tells what phonemes (of that language) are produced and in what sequence. A phonological transcription contains a symbol for each phoneme. Phonological transcriptions of the same English words are:

/pɪn/ /spɪn/ /spɪt/ /bɪt/

The phonetic transcription shows nasalized and non-nasalized vowels; the phonological transcription does not since these are not in contrast in English. The phonetic transcription indicates aspirated and unaspirated plosives, but the phonological transcription does not. And of course the phonological transcription shows that *pin* and *bit* begin with different consonants – different phonemes – and that *spin* and *spit* end with different phonemes.

When linguists describe the sound system of a language, they make a general inventory of all the phones that are produced by speakers of that language in their typical utterances. Then they decide which phones are in contrast and which are not. They decide that those which contrast are members of different phonemes and those which are similar but do not contrast are members of the same phoneme (allophones).

These statements may give the impression that phonological analysis is quite simple, but there are problems, and because there are problems, there are also different ways of analyzing. The contrast of two phonemes may be quite obvious in some contexts but not in others. Compare these two groups of English words:

beat seen feast cheap each leak
bit   sin   fist   chip   itch lick

These are **minimal pairs**. They establish that the vowel of *beat* etc. and the vowel of *bit* etc. are different phonemes. But what about the last vowel in these words?

baby cookie spaghetti

Do these words end with the vowel of *beat* or the vowel of *bit*? Some speakers of English will answer one way and other speakers will give the opposite answer. The simple fact is that in a final unstressed syllable there is no contrast; it would be impossible to find two English words that had these two vowels contrasting in final unstressed position. Some linguists would say that in this position the vowel is neither one phoneme nor the other, but the neutralization of the contrast.

We can observe the same phenomenon with high back vowels. Speakers of English will generally agree that *food, boot, Luke* have a different vowel phoneme from *good, put, look*. But what about the final vowel of *value, sinew, continue*? What is pronounced may be the vowel of *food* or the vowel of *good* and different speakers of English will make different identifications. From the point of view of a system of contrasts we can say that what occurs in final unstressed positions is the neutralization of these two phonemes. Chapters 5 and 6 deal more extensively with the matter of vowel contrasts.

Now, let's return to the three nasal consonants, /m n ŋ/. We noted their contrast in word-final position, in *rum, run, rung*, for example. We can also find contrasts in word-medial position, between vowels, as in *hammer, banner, hangar*. In word-initial position only /m/ and /n/ occur (*mail* and *nail*, for example); /ŋ/ does not. Before other consonants we have recognized a number of nasal phones, as in these words:

limp   symphony   tenth   lint   pinch   link

We can observe another fact: when a nasal consonant occurs before another consonant in word-final position, it is **homorganic** with that consonant – articulated with the same articulator and place of articulation: bilabial before /p/, labiodental before /f/, and so on. In English there is no possibility of a word like */lɪmk/ or */lɪŋt/ or */lɪnp/. (The asterisk marks a non-existent word.) So English has three nasal consonant phonemes but before another consonant in word-final position the contrast is neutralized.

FLUENCY PRACTICE 3.2

For each word in the left-hand column there is a transcription in the right-hand column. However, slant lines and square brackets have been left off. For each word, tell whether the transcription is phonetic or phonological and explain your answer.

sell	sɛɫ
sand	sænd
kiss	kʰɪs
stem	stɛ̃m
tap	tæp

LOOKING BACK

Every language has a limited inventory of phonemes, the units of its sound system. Phonemes combine in certain possible sequences to express morphemes, the units of meaning in the language. Phonemes contrast with one another to differentiate morphemes from one another. Speakers know these facts without necessarily being fully conscious of them.

A phoneme is pronounced differently in different positions of occurrence; so it is not a single speech sound but a class of speech sounds that do not contrast with one another; these speech sounds are the allophones of that phoneme. Any speech sound has certain phonetic features. The allophones of a phoneme share some of these features – the distinctive features – and differ in other features – which are redundant features. Two (or more) phonemes may share some of their distinctive features but could not contrast – could not be different phonemes – if they shared all distinctive features.

Phonemes combine with other phonemes in sequence to express morphemes, and because they enter into such sequences they contrast with other phonemes, thus serving to differentiate morphemes. In English *glue* is different from *clue* in one way – the initial phonemes are different; *glue* differs from *grew* because the second phonemes are in contrast; *glue* differs from *glee* due to the contrast of vowel phonemes. On the other hand, the vowels of *glue* and *gloom*, though phonetically different, are not in contrast and are allophones of the same phoneme. Similarly, the initial consonant of *loot* and the final consonant of *tool* are different phones but members of the same phoneme. To describe the sound system of English means to establish the phonemes of the language, to tell in what possible sequences they can occur, and what varying pronunciations each phoneme has in its various positions of occurrence.

Suggested readings

Katamba (1989) is an excellent introduction to principles of phonology. Somewhat more technical and theoretical but very readable is Spencer (1996).

Notes

The way listeners apparently process the utterances they hear is described in Clark and Clark (1977: 43ff.).

It is important to recognize that a particular symbol used to designate a phone does not necessarily have the same meaning when it is used to designate a phoneme. For example, [p] is a voiceless bilabial unaspirated plosive and [pʰ] is a voiceless bilabial aspirated plosive (in whatever languages these sounds may occur); the terms 'voiceless,' 'bilabial,' etc. indicate phonetic features. The English phoneme /p/ is a voiceless labial plosive. Here the terms 'voiceless,' 'labial,' and 'plosive' are distinctive features; they indicate the phonetic features that distinguish /p/ from other phonemes, but aspiration is not a distinctive feature in English. There is more about distinctive features in the next two chapters.

Chapter 4

English consonants

- **4.1 Distinctive features**   50
- **4.2 Consonant allophones**   56

LOOKING AHEAD

Chapter 2 introduced two kinds of obstruent consonants, plosives and fricatives, and two kinds of sonorant consonants, nasals and liquids. Chapter 3 introduced the concepts of phoneme, allophone, and distinctive features. This chapter presents an inventory of English consonant phonemes, their allophones, and their distinctive features. Section 4.1 takes up the distinctive features under these headings: manners of articulation; articulators; the voiced/voiceless contrast; and tongue shape. Section 4.2 surveys consonant allophones.

4.1 Distinctive features

According to manner of articulation we classify English consonant phonemes this way:

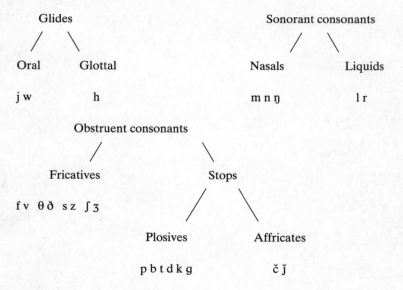

The oral glides are /j/ as in *yet* and /w/ as in *wet*. Phonetically these are vowels, high front unrounded and high back rounded, respectively, as you can verify by saying [i-ɛt] and [u-ɛt] repeatedly, making the first segment faster each time, until you are pronouncing *yet* and *wet*, respectively. Though phonetically vowels, /j/ and /w/ have the position of consonants in a syllable, just like the initial consonants of *pet*, *bet*, *met*. However, unlike /p b m/ and other consonants, they occur only at the beginning of a syllable, never in final position.

The glottal glide is /h/ as in *head*. In Chapter 2 we described this as a glottal fricative. However, within the English phonological system /h/ has a unique place. English has four pairs of fricatives articulated in the mouth, each pair consisting of one voiceless and one voiced consonant. /h/ does not belong to such a pair; it is typically voiceless though it can be voiced when it is between vowels, as in *ahead*. And /h/ is like /j/ and /w/ in that it occurs only in syllable-initial position, not at the end of a syllable. /j/ is the front oral glide and /w/ the back oral glide.

The two phonemes classified as liquids, /l/ and /r/, are characterized especially by their tongue shapes. The lateral /l/ is articulated with the sides of the tongue drawn in so that air is somewhat obstructed by the center of the tongue but passes around the sides. English /r/ is articulated with a slight groove in the tongue-tip while the body of the tongue is drawn back and humped up.

Liquids and nasals are 'musical' like vowels. Although the air stream is obstructed in some way, the vocal tract still acts as a resonance chamber in which air particles flow in periodic waves. Obstruent consonants – plosives and fricatives – are articulated with total or near-total obstruction of the air stream so that resonance is absent, in plosives, or minimal, in fricatives. For liquids and fricatives air flows out of the mouth during articulation; thus any of these consonants can be held – continued – as long as the lungs provide air. Nasals can also be prolonged since air escapes during their articulation, but through the nasal cavity alone. A plosive, since it involves complete obstruction of the breath stream, is essentially an instant of silence. A plosive can be prolonged only in the sense that the silence is maintained for a longer period of time.

There are two kinds of fricatives made with the tongue. The apicodental fricatives are articulated with a flat tongue surface, whereas /s z ʃ ʒ/ are sibilant, produced with a groove or channel along the center line of the tongue surface. Sibilant fricatives are more audible than flat fricatives because the air stream is moving through a channel which has more depth than width. Compare the final sounds of *faith* and *face*, of *bathe* and *bays*.

The consonants /č/ and /ǰ/ are affricates. An affricate is a combination of plosive and fricative. To produce the first and last consonants of *church* and *judge*, for instance, the lamina, with a groove along the centerline, makes contact with the alveolar ridge, stopping the flow of air; then the tongue is lowered and air passes along the groove, creating friction. If the tongue-front does not make contact but is positioned near the alveolar ridge, only friction occurs. Compare /č/ and /ʃ/, as in *witch* and *wish*; compare /ǰ/ and /ʒ/, as in *pledger* and *pleasure*.

English has three nasal phonemes, four pairs of fricative phonemes, and four pairs of stop phonemes. For all of them there is obstruction of the air stream in the mouth and the obstruction is caused by one of four articulators: the lower lip, the apex, the lamina, or the dorsum. Figure 4.1 is adapted from the more general chart in Chapter 2. Nasals are on the top line, plosives on the second line, and fricatives on the third line. The place of articulation is not distinctive for liquids, so /l/ and /r/ are not in the diagram.

The positions of symbols along the lines indicate norms for articulation. As we have seen, the place of articulation for any consonant (or any vowel) may vary depending on its position with respect to other phonemes. These variations are explored in Section 4.2. While the place of articulation varies, the articulator is always the same, and so we classify these consonants by the articulator.

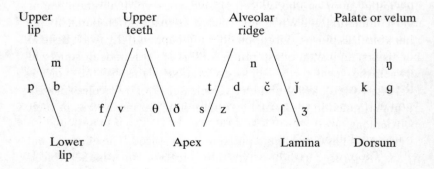

FIGURE 4.1

	Fricative	*Stop*	*Nasal*
Labial	f v	p b	m
Apical	θ ð s z	t d	n
Laminal	ʃ ʒ	č ǰ	
Dorsal		k g	ŋ

The place of articulation does not vary much for fricatives. /f/ and /v/ are labiodental: the lower lip rests lightly against the cutting edge of the upper teeth. For /θ and /ð/ the tongue-tip is near the same position (apicodental articulation). For /s/ and /z/ the tongue-tip and the front part of the lamina are close to the front of the alveolar ridge. /ʃ/ and /ʒ/ are articulated with the lamina near the back of the alveolar ridge.

Stop and fricative phonemes exist in pairs. Within each pair one phoneme is voiceless and the other is voiced. However, the terms 'voiceless' and 'voiced' don't have exactly the same meaning for fricatives and plosives. When we say that the fricative /f/ is voiceless and /v/ is voiced, we mean that the vocal cords do not vibrate during the articulation of /f/ in *feel*, *coffee*, and *leaf*, for example, and that the vocal cords do vibrate for the articulation of /v/ in, for instance, *veal*, *cover*, and *leave*. Similarly, a comparison of the plosives /p/ and /b/ between vowels, as in *rapid* and *rabid*, demonstrates that vocal cords do not vibrate in the articulation of /p/ and do vibrate when /b/ is articulated. However, for the articulation of /p/ and /b/ in initial position the difference is not in vocal cord vibration during the articulation of these plosives but rather in **voice onset time**. In the articulation of plosives the air stream is held back by the lips or tongue, so that no vibration occurs. When the air stream is released after initial /b/ or another voiced plosive, vocal cord vibration begins almost immediately. When the release is made after initial /p/ or other voiceless plosive, vibration does not happen right away. Instead there is first an instant of aspiration – a sort of [h] sound, air squeezed between the vocal cords – before vibration begins. So the 'voicedness' of a voiced plosive and the 'voicelessness' of a voiceless plosive are not so much in the actual articulation of the plosives as in their environment.

English nasal and liquid phonemes are voiced. The glides /j/ and /w/ are also voiced and /h/ is typically voiceless. But whether voiced or voiceless, the feature 'voicing' is not distinctive for these consonant phonemes since there is no contrast in English between, for example, a voiceless labial nasal and a voiced labial nasal. A feature that is not distinctive is redundant.

We have already noted that the liquid [r] is made with the tongue drawn back and bunched up and there is a slight groove in the tip. We describe this articulation by saying that [r] is a retroflex liquid. Another liquid is /l/ as in *lie* and *rely*. Compare what you do in pronouncing the /d/ of *die* and the /l/ of *lie*. For both articulations you should have the tongue-tip against the alveolar ridge. When articulating – or getting ready to articulate – /d/, you can feel your upper back teeth with the sides of your tongue. For the articulation of /l/ this is impossible. The sides of the tongue are drawn in so that air passes around the sides.

Tongue shape is also important for the sibilant fricatives /s z ʃ ʒ/ and the affricates /č ǰ/.

At this point we summarize the previous section on manner, articulator, voice, and tongue shape by giving definitions of the twenty-four consonant phonemes of English.

/p/	voiceless labial plosive
/b/	voiced labial plosive
/t/	voiceless apical plosive
/d/	voiced apical plosive
/č/	voiceless laminal plosive
/ǰ/	voiced laminal plosive
/k/	voiceless dorsal plosive
/g/	voiced dorsal plosive
/f/	voiceless labial fricative
/v/	voiced labial fricative
/θ/	voiceless apical fricative
/ð/	voiced apical fricative
/s/	voiceless apical sibilant fricative
/z/	voiced apical sibilant fricative
/ʃ/	voiceless laminal (sibilant) fricative
/ʒ/	voiced laminal (sibilant) fricative
/m/	labial nasal
/n/	apical nasal
/ŋ/	dorsal nasal
/l/	lateral liquid
/r/	retroflex liquid
/j/	front oral glide
/w/	back oral glide
/h/	glottal glide

1 Referring to the list above, what is the difference in features between:

(a) /b/ and /p/   (d) /ǰ/ and /č/

(b) /b/ and /m/   (e) /ǰ/ and /ʒ/

(c) /b/ and /v/   (f) /z/ and /ʒ/

2 In what feature(s) does /d/ differ from the following?

/t/	/ð/
/n/	/b/
/ǰ/	/g/

3 Write the symbol for the initial phoneme in each of the following words. The first is done as an example.

/z/	zebra	giant
	coral	whole
	yard	shame
	write	phrase
	water	though
	ceiling	guest

4 Each of the following words has a single consonant between vowels. Write the symbol for the medial consonant in each. The first is done as an example.

/v/	never	leather
	pageant	nature
	method	reason
	gingham	ticket
	measure	robin
	listen	patient

4.2 Consonant allophones

We recognize two kinds of variation in phonemes. (1) An allophone has some non-distinctive feature which is like the feature of a preceding or following phoneme. For example, the phoneme /m/ becomes labiodental [ɱ] like /f/ when it occurs before that consonant, as in *symphony*, whereas it is bilabial in all other environments. (2) A phoneme has different allophones in different positions in a syllable or in a word, without regard for what phoneme precedes or follows. For example, the phoneme /l/ is 'clear' before vowels as in *let* and *play* and 'dark' after vowels as in *bell* and *milk*.

The first kind is a sort of assimilation, which may be in place of articulation, as in this case, or in voice, lip shape, or tongue shape.

(a)   Since plosives and nasals require complete closure, the place of articulation is often modified by a following or preceding phoneme. The labial consonants /p b/, as well as /m/, are typically bilabial but are likely to be articulated with the lower lip against the upper teeth before labiodental /f/: *cupful, obvious*. Apical consonants such as /n t d/ are apicoalveolar in most occurrences but they are apicodental before apicodental /θ/ and /ð/: *tenth, in there, eighth, at that, width, had them*. Dorsal consonants /ŋ k g/, as mentioned in Chapter 2, have a more forward (dorsopalatal) articulation before or after front vowels: *sing, kick, giggle*; and more back (dorsovelar) articulation before and after back vowels: *song, cook, goggles*.

(b)   Consonants are articulated with the lip shape, rounded or unrounded, of the glide or vowel that follows; note the shape of your lips as you prepare to pronounce the first consonant of these words, for instance: *sue, see*; *doom, deem*; *twelve, tell*.

(c)   Obstruents are articulated with the tongue shape of a following /l/ or /r/; compare the shape of your tongue (and lips) as you get ready to pronounce the first consonant of *bay, blade, brave*, for example.

(d) Sonorant consonants and glides are likely to have a **voiceless onset** after voiceless consonants; that is, as their articulation begins, the vocal cords are not yet vibrating. Listen carefully and compare the sound of /l/ in *clay* and *glaze*, of /r/ in *pride* and *bride*, of /w/ in *twin* and *dwindle*, of /j/ in *few* and *view*.

(e) The influences of phonemes can be mutual; for example, in *play* and *crate* the plosives /p/ and /k/ are articulated with the tongue shape of the liquids /l/ and /r/, respectively, and the liquids have a voiceless onset because of the voiceless plosives. A special case of mutual influence is the following: /r/ has fricative articulation after /t/ and /d/, as in *train*, *strain*, *drain*. Here /t/ and /d/ are articulated with the slight apical groove that is characteristic of /r/. When the tongue-tip is released from the alveolar ridge, air moves through the groove creating friction. Therefore the combinations /tr/ and /dr/ are much like affricates. Compare *train* and *chain*, *drain* and *Jane*. Note the difference in the position of the tongue in the mouth and the position of the groove on the tongue.

English consonants also show variation according to position within a syllable or a word. In part, these show variation in 'strength.' Consonants in initial position are articulated with more force than those in final position, and initial position in a stressed syllable is likely to be more forceful than initial in an unstressed syllable.

(a) The lateral consonant /l/ is 'dark' when it comes after the vowel of a syllable (is part of a syllable coda, to use a term to be introduced in Chapter 6) and 'clear' when it precedes the vowel of a syllable (is part of a syllable onset).

bell   belt   waltz
live   blade

A 'dark *l*,' as we saw in Chapter 3, is made with the back of the tongue raised; the center is low; the front may be raised, so that the tongue has a spoon-like shape. A 'clear *l*' is articulated with the tongue-front high and the back low.

Between vowels, as in the following words, /l/ may be more 'dark' or more 'light,' varying with speakers.

silly valley color solid wallet

(b)   Voiceless plosives /p t k/ are aspirated in the initial position of a word or of a stressed syllable.

pie pry ply perhaps repeat depress comply
tie try tobacco detain subtract
kind cry climb canoe become decry decline

Compare, without aspiration:

spy   aspire   copy
sty   astound   city
sky   describe ticket

The affricate /č/ as in *child* is also aspirated but the friction produced in the mouth is more audible than the friction made between the vocal cords.

(c)   When voiced obstruents occur at the beginning of a word – better, perhaps, at the beginning of a tone unit – vocal cord vibration does not begin immediately; these consonants have a voiceless onset. We can represent initial /b/, for example, as [ᵖb], and similarly with the other voiced obstruents. In absolute final position vocal cord vibration may stop before the articulation is complete, so that there is a voiceless release. Final /b/ is [bᵖ], and so on.

baby daisy jade game vain those zone
tribe fade page vague save bathe is

(d)   When a plosive occurs in final position, the closure made by the lower lip or tongue is not necessarily released, e.g. *map*, *tub*, *bat*, *bed*, *book*, *pig*. When one of these consonants is syllable-final and the next syllable begins with a plosive, nasal, or /l/, the syllable-final plosive does not have separate release – its release coincides with the onset of the next consonant; the /t/ of *atlas* has lateral release, the /d/ of *kidney* has nasal release, for example. (The following consonant does not 'cause' this phenomenon; plosive release is physically possible before the next articulation but such release is just not typical of English.)

help me badly right now actor vagueness

(e) Voiceless plosives and /č/ in syllable-final position before another plosive, fricative, or nasal may be **glottalized** in some dialects. The vocal cords come together just before, or simultaneously with, the closure that occurs in the oral cavity.

help me right now each pair look fast

Some speakers may, in fact, articulate no consonant in the mouth but have only a glottal stop in this position.

(f) In the western part of England, in North America, Australia, and sporadically elsewhere, /t/ and /d/ may be articulated as **taps** when they occur between a strong vowel (and /r/) and a weak vowel.

city lady party sturdy

The tongue-tip brushes against the alveolar ridge but does not stay there long enough for air pressure to build up, as plosive articulation requires. Tapping may occur when word-final /t/ or /d/ is followed by a word-initial vowel, even if the word-inital vowel is stronger.

at all get off paid out

Many North Americans articulate a nasalized tap as the realization of the sequence /nt/ between a stronger and a weaker vowel in the same word or in word-final position closely followed by a word-initial vowel even when the latter word has greater stress.

plenty winter sent out

PRACTICE 4.2

Aspiration of voiceless plosives /p t k/ means that when the lower lip, tongue-tip, or tongue-back is released in the mouth, the vocal cords are close together and air escapes between them, producing a voiceless fricative [h]: [pʰ], [tʰ], [kʰ]. To demonstrate aspiration, hold a small strip of paper loosely in front of your mouth as you pronounce words with initial /p t k/, like the examples in paragraph (b), above, and words with medial /p t k/ before a stressed vowel. The paper should flutter because of the aspiration – most obviously with /p/ since the release of lips is most observable. Then try words that begin with /s/ plus a plosive – *spy*, *sty*, *sky*, for example. Finally, practice these three plosives in final position – *tap*, *tat*, *tack* will do – with aspiration and without.

Practice making a 'clear l' in coda position (*tell*, *ball*, *milk*, etc.), a 'dark l' in onset position (*lake*, *lot*, *claim*), and both clear and dark in medial position (*melon*, *color*, *dolly*).

LOOKING BACK

English has twenty-four consonant phonemes, distinguished from one another, first, by manner of articulation, which determines five groups – stops, fricatives, nasals, liquids, and glides. Within each group other kinds of features are distinctive, as follows:

Eight stops are distinguished from one another by voice and by four kinds of articulators, labial /b p/, apical /d t/, laminal (ǰ č), and dorsal (g k).

Eight fricatives are distinguished from one another by voice; by three articulators, labial /v f/, apical /ð θ z s/, and laminal /ʒ ʃ/; and by tongue shape, sibilant /z s ʒ ʃ/ and flat /ð θ/.

Three nasals are distinguished from one another by type of articulator, labial /m/, apical /n/, dorsal /ŋ/.

Two liquids are distinguished by tongue shape: lateral /l/ and retroflex /r/.

Three glides are distinguished as front oral glide /j/, back oral glide /w/, and glottal glide /h/.

In all languages some things are distinctive and some are redundant, and some are sometimes distinctive and sometimes redundant. In English grammar there is a distinction between singular and plural in nouns, so that *the house* and *the houses* are obviously different. But in *five houses* the plural suffix *-s* is redundant; plurality is expressed more precisely and sufficiently by the number *five*. Similarly, in *We played tennis yesterday* the past tense suffix *-ed* is redundant, although without any time word like *yesterday* the difference between *we played* and *we play* is an important grammatical distinction.

Phonology also has redundancy. Every speech sound is either voiced or voiceless, but in English voicing is distinctive for obstruent consonants and redundant for sonorant consonants. It is not always simple to say what feature is distinctive and what is redundant. The glide /j/ is front and unrounded, /w/ is back and rounded. We might equally well say that tongue position is distinctive and lip-rounding is redundant, or that lip-rounding is distinctive and tongue position redundant.

A phoneme, we need to remember, is an abstract unit. It has actual, concrete pronunciations that are different – allophones – in different contexts. Some allophonic differences are assimilatory – the pronunciation includes non-distinctive features similar to features of neighboring phonemes – point of articulation, tongue shape, lip shape, and so on. Such assimilations seem natural and are, to some degree, universal. Other allophonic differences are language-specific and involve differences of occurrence within a word, a syllable, or in stressed versus unstressed syllables. In English the voiceless plosives /p t k/ are aspirated in word-initial position and before a stressed vowel. After /s/ and before an unstressed vowel they are unaspirated. In word-final position they may be aspirated or not. When the aspirated allophones [pʰ tʰ kʰ] occur in certain positions and the unaspirated allophones [p t k] occur in other positions, the allophones are said to be in **complementary distribution**. When either the aspirated or the unaspirated allophones may occur, as in word-final position, they are in **free variation**. At any rate, the occurrence of aspirated or unaspirated phones has nothing to do with neighboring phonemes. Similarly, there is no physical reason why the phoneme /l/ should have a clear allophone before a vowel and a dark allophone after, or why it should have two such different allophones at all.

Suggested readings

Somewhat different treatments of English consonants are found in Ladefoged (1993: Chapter 3) and Roach (1991: Chapters 4, 6, and 7).

Notes

1   The symbol for a phoneme is often the same as the phonetic symbol that represents its most common pronunciation, but this is not necessarily the case; a phone is a specific speech element while a phoneme is an abstract unit in the system of contrasts of a particular language. The affricates in *church* and *judge* are represented phonetically as [ʧ] and [ʤ], respectively, where the [t] and [d] indicate the closure made with the tongue and [ʃ] and [ʒ] the fricative release. Some phonologists represent the phonemes with the same symbols, thus /ʧ/ and /ʤ/. Others take the point of view adopted here: that the affricates, while phonetically compound, are phonologically single elements in a series of four pairs of stops: /p b t d č ǰ k g/.

   A related but more complex question of interpretation is this: can the affricates be interpreted, not as single phonemes but as sequences of two phonemes, /t/ plus /ʃ/ and /d/ plus /ʒ/. A succinct treatment of the question can be found in Lass (1984: 26–7).

2   The fricative /ʒ/ and the nasal /ŋ/ are more restricted than other fricatives and nasals. /ʒ/ occurs in word-initial position in foreign names like *Giselle* or *Zhivago* but not in native English words. It is frequent between vowels (e.g. *leisure, occasion, vision*), less common in word-final position (e.g. *beige, garage, rouge*) where some speakers substitute the affricate /ǰ/. /ŋ/ does not occur word-initially. It is rare between vowels (*dinghy, gingham, hangar* and names like *Bingham*); otherwise it occurs only before /k/ (e.g. *bank, drunkard, think*), before /g/ (e.g. *angry, finger, single*), and at the end of morphemes (e.g. *thing, gangster, sing-er*; see Chapter 8 for an explanation of **morpheme**). Some speakers pronounce a plosive /g/ in *gingham, thing, singer*, etc. Therefore, in their dialects the dorsal nasal does not have the status of a phoneme. It is the allophone of /n/ that occurs only before /g/ and /k/.

3　The consonant /r/ has a fricative quality when following /t/ or /d/ and, as noted above, the sequences /tr/ and /dr/ are similar perceptually to affricates /č/ and /ǰ/, respectively. In rhotic dialects a syllabic [r̩] may also be fricative after /t/ and /d/, as in *shelter*, *murder*, *terrain*, *Mediterranean*, *militaristic*. The sequence of [tr̩] is acoustically somewhat similar to an aspirated [tʰ].

Chapter 5

English vowels

- **5.1 Dialect differences** 66
- **5.2 A general inventory of vowels** 69
- **5.3 Vowel inventories of specific English dialects** 80

LOOKING AHEAD

Describing the vowel phonemes of English is more difficult than describing the consonant phonemes because the various dialects of the language have somewhat different vowels. (We use the word vowel as a cover term to include monophthong, diphthong, or triphthong). In Section 5.1 these variations are described as differences of **inventory**, **incidence**, and **pronunciation**.

Section 5.2 introduces a general inventory of twenty-four key words, each with a vowel that differs from all the others in some variety of English though not necessarily in all varieties. The twenty-four key words are divided into those that have a **checked vowel**, those that have a **free vowel**, and those that have an **R-vowel**. Pronunciation diagrams show how these are realized.

The chapter concludes with representative inventories of vowels in several different varieties of English (Section 5.3).

5.1 Dialect differences

Chapter 2 described different kinds of consonant articulations and Chapter 4 treated the consonant phonemes of English. The two topics were related but not the same. A phoneme, as we have seen, is not a single phone – a single articulation in a particular part of the mouth – but a group of phones that are alike in some features but different in others. Dealing with vowel phones and vowel phonemes is likewise a double task. Chapter 2 introduced the cardinal vowels as points in the mouth that can be used for reference in describing other vowels. However, when we describe the vowel phonemes of English – or any language – we are not dealing with points but with areas. When you pronounce the words *pit*, *fish*, *bill*, and *spirit*, for instance, it is quite unlikely that your tongue is in exactly the same place for the pronunciation of the (stressed) vowel in these words. X-ray photographs would possibly show four different locations – dots that are close to one another, of course, but by no means the same. And if we bring together several people from different parts of the English-speaking world and make X-ray pictures as they pronounce these four words, the dots would cover a still bigger area. However, if we compare the (stressed) vowels of these words with the (stressed) vowels of *pet*, *flesh*, *bell*, *merit*, spoken by one person or a number of speakers, we will see that a constant relationship exists: the vowel of *pit* is to the vowel of *pet* as the vowel of *fish* is to the vowel of *flesh*, and so on; the vowel phones of *pit*, *fish*, *bill*, *spirit* are generally made in the high front part of the mouth, and the vowel phones of *pet*, *flesh*, *bell*, *merit* in the mid front area.

Describing English vowel phonemes is more difficult than describing the consonant phonemes. The **inventory**, or total number, of consonant phonemes is the same in all varieties of English, twenty-four. The **phonetic realizations**, or pronunciations, of these consonants differ relatively little from one group of speakers to another. There are some small differences regarding the **incidence** of consonants – that is, which consonants occur in specific words; for instance, *greasy* has /z/ in the middle for some speakers, /s/ for others, but such differences are trivial.

When we consider English vowels, we find that different dialects of the language differ from one another in just these ways: inventory, phonetic realizations, and incidence. How is it possible that speakers of a language do not all make the same vowel differences? The answer is that language is always changing and a change may happen in some places, or among some groups of people, but may not happen everywhere.

For most speakers of English today the words *put*, *bush*, *full*, and *wolf* have one vowel and the words *nut*, *rush*, *sun*, and *young* have a different vowel, but it was not always so. Originally all these words had the same vowel; *nut* rhymed with *put*, and *rush* rhymed with *bush*. At some time – probably in the seventeenth century – the phoneme 'split'; what were different pronunciations in different contexts – different allophones – came, for a complex of reasons, to occur in the same context, that is, came to be contrasting phonemes. However, in the north of England the split did not occur; there all of the words listed above, and of course many others, have the same vowel, and so there is one less vowel in the inventory of phonemes than in dialects that have incorporated this split.

Difference of inventory may be due to another kind of change, a merger. Some Canadians and Americans now have the same vowel phoneme in *cot*, *lock*, *pond* as in *caught*, *hawk*, *pawn* whereas the two vowel phonemes are distinct for most speakers. Ordinary people are aware that others speak differently from the way they themselves speak but they are not aware of just what these differences are.

Dialects differ in the incidence of phonemes because there has been both split and merger, or the split has affected different lexical items in different dialects. The words *cat*, *calf*, *car*, *call* originally had the same vowel. This vowel diverged in all dialects of English, but in quite different ways in different dialects. A number of words like *calf* have the same vowel as *cat* for some speakers, the same vowel as *car* for others. Exhibit 5.1 gives more examples of this.

EXHIBIT 5.1 ──

Most Irish, Scots, Canadians, and Americans have /æ/ in the following words, where speakers of RP have /ɑ/. Other British dialects and those of the Caribbean, Australia, New Zealand, and South Africa are like RP in this regard, with some exceptions. This situation results from a change that occurred perhaps in the eighteenth century. In southern England the low front vowel came to be pronounced farther back and long before the voiceless consonants /f θ s/ when these consonants were word-final or pre-consonantal – illustrated in 1, 2, and 3, respectively. /ɑ/ occurs less regularly before the corresponding voiced fricatives (4). At a later time the low front vowel was retracted before a nasal followed by a front consonant (5).

1   after, calf, craft, draft, giraffe, half, laugh, photograph, staff;
2   bath, path, wrath;
3   ask, basket, brass, (broad)cast, castle, clasp, class, disaster, fast, fasten, glass, grass, grasp, last, mask, nasty, pass, past, pastor, plaster, task, vast;
4   calve, halve, raspberry, rather;
5   advance, answer, aunt, branch, can't, chant, command, dance, example, France, glance, grant, plant, sample, transport.

1 Pronounce the words *bib*, *did*, *gig*. Notice the position of your tongue for the vowel in each of the three words. How similar and how different are these positions?

2 Compare these vowels followed by /t/ and followed by /l/: *bet*, *bell*; *pat*, *pal*; *seat*, *seal*; *fate*, *fail*; *boat*, *bowl*; *mite*, *mile*; *out*, *owl*. How does the presence of /l/ affect the pronunciation of the vowels?

3 Compare the length of vowels before voiceless and voiced consonants, as in *bit*, *bid*; *cap*, *cab*; *lake*, *vague*; *rice*, *rise*. In which position are vowels longer? (It's best to put these in a context in order to make an accurate judgement – something like "Can you spell *bit?*" "Can you spell *bid?*" – taking pairs of words in random order.

5.2 A general inventory of vowels

Vowels can differ from one another in several ways. The most important is quality – determined mostly by the position of the tongue in the mouth, higher or lower, more forward or more back. Figure 5.1 shows how twelve vowels compare in quality – that is, in their relative positions in the mouth. We use key words in Figure 5.1 and throughout this chapter to designate these vowels, and other key words are introduced below.

In addition to key words we want to designate vowel phonemes with symbols. If we were dealing with a single dialect of English, each vowel phoneme would be pronounced in more or less the same way by all speakers of the dialect and our symbol for each vowel phoneme could be the symbol for the phonetic norm. In dealing with the vowel phonemes of different dialects, our symbols for these phonemes are necessarily more abstract, less phonetic. For example, the vowels of DAY and TIE are pronounced quite differently by different speakers. We represent these phonologically as /dei/ and /tai/, respectively. The vowel symbols chosen are phonetically fairly accurate for what some speakers pronounce and less accurate for what other speakers say. The essential point is that /ei/, /ai/, and the ways of symbolizing other vowel phonemes are simply labels. The detail of pronunciation are in Section 5.3.

In addition to quality, vowel phonemes can also differ in length, some typically longer than others. They can differ too in complexity; monophthongs are made with the tongue motionless, diphthongs with the tongue moving – and triphthongs, which we discuss later, involve two movements of the tongue. Four of the key words in Figure 5.1 have vowels that are long or diphthongal or both, depending on dialect. We now introduce the symbols that we will use for these key vowels.

TREE /ii/   TRUE /uu/
DAY /ei/   TOE /ou/

If TREE and DAY are pronounced as diphthongs, the front of the tongue moves upward, and when TRUE and TOE are diphthongs, the back of the tongue moves upward. Of course, the higher the vowel that begins the dipthong, the less room there is for upward movement.

Three more key words contain vowels that are typically diphthongs:

TIE /ai/   NOW /au/   TOY /oi/

TIE and TOY are fronting diphthongs – the tongue-front moves upward – and NOW is a backing diphthong – the back of the tongue moves up. Details about pronunciations come later, along with diagrams.

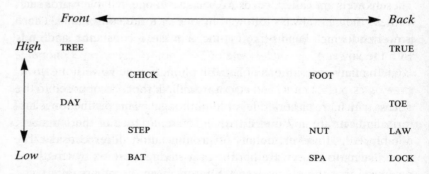

FIGURE 5.1 Comparative positions for twelve vowels

Two key words in Figure 5.1 have long vowels:

LAW /ɔ/   SPA /ɑ/

That makes a total of nine vowels that are either diphthongs or long. They are also relatively tense, made with tongue (and lip) muscles relatively tense, in contrast to the other six vowels to be discussed below.

These nine are also **free vowels**; they can occur at the end of a word, as in the key words themselves, or followed by one or two consonants within the same syllable; for example:

TREE	treat, leak, deep, niece, least, even, machine
DAY	date, fade, chain, wage, change, favor, parade
TRUE	fruit, smooth, choose, pool, boost, prudent, recruit
TOE	boat, hope, choke, vogue, toast, holy, remote
TIE	light, wide, nice, type, pint, silent, polite
NOW	out, loud, house, down, bounce, county, about
TOY	void, voice, coin, noise, moist, oyster, appoint,
LAW	caught, laud, cause, sauce, false, caution, applause
SPA	calm, father, façade

The six remaining vowels are relatively lax and they are **checked vowels**. To repeat the key words and introduce symbols for these vowels:

CHICK	/ɪ/	FOOT	/ʊ/
STEP	/ɛ/	NUT	/ʌ/
BAT	/æ/	LOCK	/ɒ/

These vowels are called 'checked' because in one-syllable words such as these they are always followed by one or more consonants. There is no word which begins like CHICK or STEP, for instance, and ends with the vowel.

In many descriptions of English phonetics the vowels of CHICK, STEP, BAT, NUT, LOCK, and FOOT are called 'short' as opposed to the others, which are either 'long' or 'diphthongal.' This distinction is historically accurate and is still true in some varieties of the language, notably RP. However, details of pronunciation differ considerably from dialect to dialect. Rather than classifying these six by length we recognize that these vowels are different from the others on a tactic criterion: these vowels never occur in final position; they are always

71

'checked,' followed by one, two, or three consonants, as in these examples:

CHICK	lip, rib, myth, rich, glimpse, silver, omit
STEP	bet, chef, death, neck, tempt, devil, caress
BAT	tack, map, sad, latch, valve, camel, relax
FOOT	wood, push, full, hook, wolf, bullet, sugar
NUT	cup, rub, love, budge, lump, money, corrupt
LOCK	crop, hot, lodge, bomb, bronze, solid, dissolve

Dialects of English differ notably in whether there is or is not a consonant /r/ occurring in words like the following (shown with our way of symbolizing):

EAR	/ir/			TOUR	/ur/
CHAIR	/er/			DOOR	/or/
		FUR	/ɜr/		
STAR	/ar/			WAR	/ɔr/
FIRE	/air/			SOUR	/aur/

Dialects of English are labeled either 'rhotic' or 'non-rhotic.' In rhotic dialects the nine key words above are pronounced with /r/ at the end, a liquid consonant articulated with tongue retracted and a groove in the tip. In non-rhotic dialects there is no consonant. EAR, CHAIR, TOUR, and perhaps DOOR have in-gliding diphthongs, in which the tongue moves to a mid central position; TIRE and TOWER have triphthongs; FUR has a unique long vowel; CAR and WAR have long vowels identical with those of SPA and LAW, respectively. These details and illustrations of them appear in the next section.

RP and all of southeastern England, Australia, New Zealand, South Africa, and, variably, the southern United States and eastern New England are non-rhotic. Northern and western England, Scotland, Wales, Ireland, Canada, and most of the United States are rhotic, and there are groups of 'R-ful' speakers in areas which are generally non-rhotic, or 'R-less.'

For convenience we refer to the vowels of these nine key words as 'R vowels'; here are other illustrations of them:

EAR	steer, fierce, weird, weary, cheerful, appear
CHAIR	dare, scarce, stairs, dairy, careless, aware
TOUR	pure, boor, tourist, mural, furious, insure
DOOR	four, hoarse, sport, porch, mourning, adore

WAR	fork, short, corn, horse, morning, abhor
FUR	nurse, hurt, word, germ, girl, circus, absurd
STAR	bar, hard, march, charm, margin, barley, remark
FIRE	spire, tired, diary, fiery, tyrant, admire
SOUR	tower, dowry, flowery, devour

We have introduced twenty-four key words but these do not represent twenty-four different vowel phonemes. Different varieties of the language have different selections from among these twenty-four. Our next task is to describe how these are pronounced, after which we show the inventory of vowel phonemes for different dialects.

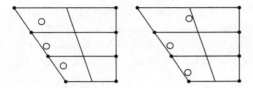

FIGURE 5.2 CHICK, STEP, BAT

CHICK, STEP, BAT are, respectively, high front, mid front, and low front in most varieties of English, as shown on the left of Figure 5.2. Thus for CHICK there is a relatively small space above the tongue and quite a large space behind it. For STEP and BAT there is greater space above the tongue. In New Zealand the vowel of CHICK is high central, as shown on the right of Figure 5.2. Some speakers, in various places, have a vowel which ranges from high front to high central, depending on what consonants are adjacent.

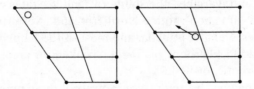

FIGURE 5.3 TREE

The vowel of TREE is higher high front and tense in the pronunciation of most speakers, either long [iː] or with tongue moving up slightly [iⁱ] (left of Figure 5.3). For some speakers in the United Kingdom and Australia the vowel begins in higher mid central position and has upward movement of the tongue-front [əⁱ] (right of Figure 5.3).

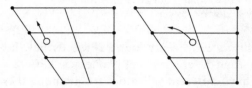

FIGURE 5.4 DAY

The vowel of DAY is generally made with the tongue-front moving upward from the mid front position [eⁱ]; in northern England, Scotland, and Ireland it may be long but non-gliding [eː]; in Cockney and Broad Australian the beginning is lower mid central and in the Caribbean higher mid central, as shown on the right of Figure 5.4.

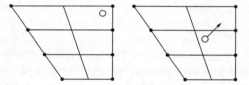

FIGURE 5.5 TRUE

The vowel of TRUE is higher high back, tense, and somewhat rounded, either long [uː] or with tongue-back moving upward [uᵘ]. It is likely to be more forward after laminal consonants (e.g. *chew, juice, shoe*) and in some dialects, notably Scots, it is high central in all positions. In Cockney and Broad Australian the vowel begins in higher mid central position and then the back of the tongue moves upward [əᵘ] (right of Figure 5.5).

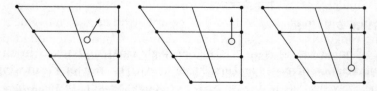

FIGURE 5.6 TOE

The vowel of TOE is generally tense and rounded with the tongue-back moving upward; in RP and the southern hemisphere the vowel begins from a mid central position, [ɜᵘ] (left of Figure 5.6), in North America from a mid back position, [oᵘ] (center); in Scotland and Ireland mid back with no appreciable tongue movement; in Cockney and Broad Australian the beginning is higher low back (right).

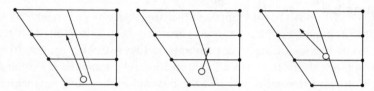

FIGURE 5.7 TIE

TIE has a variety of pronunciations, mostly beginning low front or low central followed by upward movement of the tongue-front [aⁱ] (left of Figure 5.7); in the southern United States it is [aⁱ] before voiceless consonants but [aː] or [aᵊ] elsewhere (center). For most Canadians and some Americans the vowel has a mid central beginning point [ʌⁱ] before voiceless consonants (right) and [aⁱ] elsewhere.

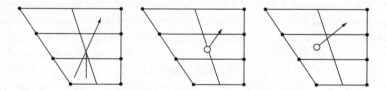

FIGURE 5.8 NOW

Similarly, NOW has a variety of pronunciations, mostly beginning in the low area, low front or low central, with upward movement of the tongue-back, [æᵘ, aᵘ] as lips change from neutral to rounded (left of Figure 5.8); Canadians and some Americans have a mid central beginning point [ʌᵘ] when the vowel occurs before a voiceless consonant (center); in Broad Australian and Cockney the beginning may be mid front, [ɛᵘ] (right).

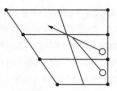

FIGURE 5.9 TOY

The vowel of TOY begins in the low back area or somewhat higher, with upward movement of the tongue-front, [ɔⁱ] as lips change from rounded to unrounded; the beginning may be somewhat higher or lower but variation is negligible. (See Figure 5.9.)

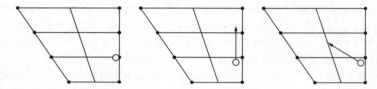

FIGURE 5.10 LAW

LAW has a long, rounded, tense vowel, which is lower mid back or higher low back in RP and the southern hemisphere (left of Figure 5.10). Two other pronunciations have movement of the tongue-back upward (center), in the speech of some southern Americans, or movement of the tongue to a mid central position (right). In Cockney the upward-gliding vowel occurs in closed syllables, the centering one in open syllables.

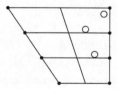

FIGURE 5.11 TRUE, FOOT, NUT

The vowel of TRUE was treated above (Figure 5.5). FOOT has a lax, high back vowel with weak rounding [ʊ], lower than TRUE. NUT is a lax unrounded vowel, higher or lower mid central (Figure 5.11). In Scotland and Northern Ireland words which elsewhere have the

FOOT vowel have the TRUE vowel instead; there is no contrast between *Luke* and *look*, for instance. For many speakers in the north of England words that elsewhere are pronounced with the vowel of NUT are pronounced instead with the vowel of FOOT. In other words, there is no contrast between *buck* and *book*, for example.

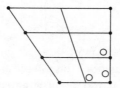

FIGURE 5.12 LAW, LOCK, SPA

In most of England, Scotland, Wales, South Africa, Australia, and New Zealand LAW is a lower mid back tense rounded vowel, SPA is low back, tense, and unrounded, and LOCK is low back, lax, and rounded (Figure 5.12). In western England, Ireland, and most of North America LOCK is an unrounded vowel, and hence SPA and LOCK are pronounced with the same vowel, and *father* rhymes with *bother*, for example. A three-vowel contrast is reduced to a two-vowel contrast. For some Americans and many Canadians LAW, LOCK, and SPA have the same low back unrounded vowel; a three-way contrast is reduced to a single vowel.

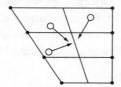

FIGURE 5.13 EAR, CHAIR, TOUR

In RP and other non-rhotic dialects these are diphthongs in which the tongue moves to mid central position; EAR starts from the high front position of CHICK, the diphthong of CHAIR begins with the mid front position of STEP, and that of TOUR from the high back position of FOOT. What is pronounced in mid central position is a non-syllabic schwa; in phonetic representation these are, respectively [ɪə ɛə ʊə] (see Figure 5.13). In rhotic dialects they are simple vowels followed by a consonant /r/, which can become syllabic. The vowels may be close to those of CHICK, STEP, FOOT, respectively (North

America) or to those of TREE, DAY, TRUE, respectively (Scotland and Ireland).

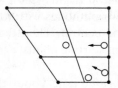

FIGURE 5.14 FUR, STAR, DOOR, WAR

In rhotic dialects the vowel of FUR is a mid central, slightly rounded, comparatively long vowel produced with the tongue drawn back and with a groove in the very tip; what is phonologically a sequence of vowel + /r/ is phonetically an R-colored vowel – the groove and tongue retraction are present throughout the pronunciation. In non-rhotic dialects the vowel is equivalent except that there is no groove or retraction. In rhotic dialects the vowel of STAR is like that of SPA followed by /r/. In non-rhotic dialects STAR and SPA rhyme; they have the same vowel. The older distinction between the vowels of DOOR and WAR is preserved in Scotland, Ireland, New England, and the American south. In rhotic varieties these are are mid back and low back rounded vowels (like TOE and LAW, respectively) followed by /r/. In non-rhotic varieties they are diphthongs beginning from the same respective positions followed by a glide to mid central [oᵊ ɔᵊ]. In RP and other dialects of England, Wales, and the southern hemisphere DOOR and WAR are identical with each other and with LAW, a low back long, rounded vowel [ɔː]. (See Figure 5.14.)

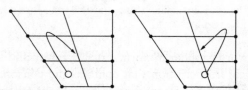

FIGURE 5.15 FIRE, SOUR

The vowels of FIRE and SOUR can be equated with those of TIE and NOW, respectively, followed by a consonant /r/ in rhotic dialects and a non-syllabic schwa in non-rhotic ones. Both begin with a low position – variably more forward or more back. In non-rhotic pronunciations the tongue then moves, for FIRE, toward the high front area and then to mid central (left); for SOUR toward the high back area and then mid central (right) (see Figure 5.15). There is a tendency to 'smooth' these triphthongs with tongue movements that go directly from low to mid central. Then they can only be distinguished if they have different starting points, e.g. [aᵊ] for FIRE, [æᵊ] for SOUR.

We need to add a further note about the R-vowels (Figures 5.13–5.15). In non-rhotic dialects there is no phoneme /r/ after any of these vowels, if the vowel is final or followed by a consonant. If any of these vowels is followed by another vowel, /r/ is pronounced. This happens within a word (e.g. *cereal*, *sorry*, *starry*) and when a word with a final R-vowel is closely linked to a following word that begins with a vowel, as in *far and near*, *near and far*, *Where is it?*, *war and peace*. Thus such words as *near*, *where*, *far*, *war*, which always have /r/ in rhotic dialects, have two pronunciations in non-rhotic dialects, one without and one with a 'linking R.' Furthermore, an 'intrusive R' may appear where there is no /r/ in rhotic dialects. Since, in non-rhotic dialects, *law* rhymes with *war* and *spa* with *star* when these are final in a phrase, they are treated in similar fashion when in the middle of a phrase: *law-r-and order*, *the spa-r-is near*.

PRACTICE 5.2

1 Here are common English words written in our transcription. Give the standard orthographic form for each.

/fɪʃ ʃiip čɛst grein blæk pɑm kʊd fruut trʌmp houst θɔ dɒk waif haus ǰoint pirs sterz gard θɜrst ʃur porč wɔrm hair aur/

2 The next words appear in normal orthography and then in a phonological transcription that contains the consonant symbols but not the symbols for vowels. Supply the missing vowel symbols.

Beth	/b θ/	these	/ð z/
patch	/p č/	large	/l ǰ/
brook	/br k/	stomp	/st mp/

crumb	/kr m/	count	/k nt/
third	/θ d/	goose	/g s/
noise	/n z/	kind	/k nd/
dear	/d /	gauze	/g z/
strict	/str kt/	quaint	/kw nt/
phone	/f n/	storm	/st m/

5.3 Vowel inventories of specific English dialects

Here is our inventory of twenty-four key words:

Checked vowels		*Free vowels*		*R-vowels*		
CHICK	FOOT	TREE		TRUE	EAR	TOUR
STEP	NUT	DAY		TOE	CHAIR FUR	DOOR
BAT	LOCK	SPA		LAW	STAR	WAR
		TIE	TOY	NOW	FIRE	SOUR

In the Republic of Ireland, a rhotic dialect area, all twenty-four of these vowel distinctions are maintained, but that does not mean that there are twenty-four vowel phonemes. The R-vowels are pronounced with a sonorant consonant and, except for FUR, they have generally the same quality as free vowels: the EAR vowel has the same quality as the vowel of TREE, CHAIR the same as DAY, FIRE the same as TIE, and so on.

The vowel system of rhotic dialects in the north of England is almost identical. The one difference is that the distinction between the vowel of FOOT and that of NUT does not exist. To put it another way, for these speakers there is no NUT vowel. The set of words represented by NUT and the set of words represented by FOOT are a single set in this variety, all having the same vowel.

The English spoken in Scotland and Northern Ireland is almost identical with that of southern Ireland, so far as number of vowel contrasts is concerned, with two exceptions: words of the FOOT class have the vowel of the TRUE class – or, to say it differently, there is no FOOT vowel; likewise, the set of words represented by BAT and the set represented by SPA are, for most Scots speakers, pronounced with the same vowel.

The next inventory shows the vowel contrasts in a broad variety of dialects: in the south of England, including RP and Cockney, in South Africa, New Zealand, and Australia. Within this range of dialects there are big differences of pronunciation – between Cockney and RP, for instance – but the vowel system is essentially the same.

CHICK	FOOT	TREE	TRUE	EAR	TOUR
STEP	NUT	DAY	TOE	CHAIR FUR	
BAT	LOCK	SPA = STAR	LAW = DOOR = WAR		
		TIE	TOY	NOW	FIRE	SOUR

The sets represented by EAR, CHAIR, and TOUR have centering diphthongs (see Figure 5.13), though for the CHAIR set a pronunciation with a long open vowel [ɛː] seems to be spreading among the younger generation of RP speakers. FUR and STAR words have long vowels, the latter being identical with SPA. The sets DOOR and WAR are identical. Among older speakers of RP LAW may have a long vowel and WAR a centering diphthong; among younger speakers the three sets – DOOR, WAR, LAW – are identical.

The next inventory may be called Conservative North American, the system of vowels in dialects spoken by many Americans and Canadians. This is a common inventory, with differences of actual pronunciation as noted earlier under Figures 5.2–5.15.

CHICK	FOOT	TREE	TRUE	EAR	TOUR
STEP	NUT	DAY	TOE	CHAIR FUR	DOOR
BAT		SPA = LOCK	LAW	STAR	WAR
		TIE	TOY	NOW	FIRE	SOUR

Within this range, eastern New England and the southern United States are mostly non-rhotic and all other areas rhotic. In rhotic dialects the vowels indicated by EAR, CHAIR, STAR, FIRE, TOUR, DOOR, WAR, SOUR are, respectively, like the vowels of CHICK, STEP, SPA, TIE, FOOT, TOE, LAW, NOW followed by /r/. In non-rhotic dialects there is a non-syllabic schwa in place of /r/.

A large – and growing – number of North Americans have no contrast between the DOOR set and the WAR set. Unlike most other varieties of English the LOCK vowel is identical with the SPA vowel. For many, and apparently an increasing number of, Canadians and Americans there is no contrast between SPA, LOCK, and LAW.

The last inventory here is one for Jamaica, which broadly represents a number of different varieties of English spoken in the Caribbean.

CHICK	FOOT	TREE		TRUE			
STEP	NUT	DAY		TOE	EAR = CHAIR FUR	TOUR = DOOR
BAT	LOCK	SPA		LAW	STAR		WAR
		TIE	TOY	NOW	FIRE		SOUR

The vowel of EAR is not distinguished from that of CHAIR in this non-rhotic variety, and there is no distinction between those of TOUR and DOOR, which, however, is distinct from WAR. The vowel of TOY is replaced by TIE in the speech of some, and the BAT and LOCK vowels may not be distinguished.

PROJECT 5.3

Using the inventory of twenty-four key words, make a description of the vowel system in your own variety of English. Is your speech rhotic or non-rhotic? Are there contrasts existing in other varieties that are not present in your dialect? Using Figures 5.2–5.15, describe the pronunciation norm(s) for each vowel phoneme in your inventory.

EXERCISE 5.4

Exhibit 5.1 showed one example of a dialect difference in vowel incidence: in words like *half, class, grant* some speakers have /ɑ/, the vowel of SPA, and others have /æ/, the vowel of BAT. Here is another difference of vowel incidence. The following words may all have the same vowel phoneme in your speech – probably the vowel of LOCK – or some may have one vowel and other words a different vowel – probably the vowels of LOCK and LAW – depending mainly on what consonant follows or how many syllables there are. Examine your pronunciation of the following words. If you have different vowel phonemes in different words, what are the environments in which each occurs? If possible, compare your findings with somebody else's.

hot top job rod frog lodge watch cough cloth loss wash bomb gone long doll laundry office sausage

LOOKING BACK

Describing English vowels is a greater task than describing the consonant phonemes of the language. The difficulty is due to the fact that different varieties of English have different vowel systems. Average speakers of English, listening to someone who comes from a different part of the English-speaking world, are likely to notice differences of pronunciation, for example, in the way the other person says *time* or *house*. Our average speakers probably also note differences of incidence; perhaps that the other person says *rather* with the vowel of *father* instead of the vowel of *gather*, or vice versa. But ordinary speakers of a language will not recognize that there are differences of inventory – that some varieties make distinctions which do not exist for other speakers.

Regarding occurrences of vowels, the most noteworthy point to be made is the distinction (in Dutch and German as well as English) between free vowels and checked vowels: certain vowels, such as the one in *bee* and *beat*, occur in both open and closed syllables, whereas other vowels, such as the one in *bit*, do not occur in final open syllables. With respect to pronunciation, free vowels are generally longer than checked vowels and/or are more likely to be diphthongal, though details vary considerably.

Dialects of English can be distinguished as 'rhotic' and 'non-rhotic.' In Early Modern times the historic phoneme /r/ ceased to be pronounced as a consonant, by some speakers, in post-vocalic position (e.g. *car, card*). It did not, however, completely disappear even in non-rhotic dialects; it is still present as length in FUR, STAR, and WAR and as a non-syllabic schwa in EAR, CHAIR, TOUR.

In spite of all the differences that must necessarily be pointed out in a discussion of English vowels, it is also necessary to recognize that 'dialects' do not exist in the pure form that might seem to be the case. In an age of great mobility such as the present, people move around, often living as adults in an area distinct from the one in which they spent their childhood and are influenced by pronunciations of new words via radio, television, or cinema from people far away. It is also important to reiterate that different varieties of the language are mutually intelligible.

Suggested readings

Wells (1982) is the standard – indeed, the only – thorough treatment of the phonology of English with attention to all native-speaker varieties. Chapter 1 offers an excellent overview of what these varieties are, how they differ, and why. The whole book invites browsing, and browsers will probably find themselves reading seriously in the portions that treat the dialects which interest them most.

The material in this chapter draws from Kreidler (1990), a more extensive treatment of dialect differences and commonalities.

Note

Linguists have made rather different analyses of English vowels and have used different sets of symbols for them, a fact that often bewilders students just beginning in linguistics. Kreidler (1989: Appendix 1) offers an explanation of why this diversity exists and compares four of the best-known systems for transcribing English vowel phonemes.

Chapter 6

Syllables

- **6.1 The structure of a syllable**   87
- **6.2 Consonants in clusters**   90
- **6.3 Inflections**   96

LOOKING AHEAD

A syllable is an important unit of speech although no one has successfully explained what a syllable is in physiological terms. It does not correspond to an impulse in the breathing process, as phoneticians once believed. Still, recognition of syllables is a fact of human history. There is no society that does not have poetry. In different cultures more importance may be given to alliteration, assonance, or rhyme, but universally poetry requires meter, specific numbers of syllables per line. Another point: syllabaries – writing systems in which each graphic unit represents a syllable – have been invented numerous times in different parts of the world, but the alphabet – one symbol per phoneme – has come into existence only once, and perhaps that was due to a series of fortunate accidents made by the Phoenicians and Greeks.

This chapter first treats the structure of a syllable (Section 6.1), introducing the terms **onset**, **nucleus**, and **coda** as general names for the components. Every language has restrictions, or **constraints**, on how its phonemes can go together in sequences; some languages permit only consonant–vowel–consonant–vowel (CVCV) etc. English has clusters of consonants which partly follow a **scale of sonority**, and these constraints are examined in Section 6.2.

Some very common grammatical suffixes, including the one that makes a noun plural and the one that makes a verb past tense, have different pronunciations. These different forms depend on the final phoneme of the noun or verb to which they are attached. Section 6.3 examines the rules that determine these different forms.

6.1 The structure of a syllable

Every syllable has a structure: it consists of certain phonemes in a particular sequence; for example, *Ned*, *den*, and *end* have the same three phonemes, /d/, /ɛ/, and /n/, but in different sequences. The words *leap*, *peel*, and *plea* consist of the same phonemes, /l/, /p/, and /ii/, in different arrangements. A word also has a structure: it consists of at least one syllable, like the six words just mentioned, and numerous words have two, three, four, or more syllables in a particular sequence. We describe the structure of a syllable by telling what phonemes it has and in what sequence they occur; we describe the structure of a word by telling what syllables it has and, if the word consists of more than one syllable, in what sequence the syllables occur and which syllable is the most prominent – the stressed syllable. We can describe the structure of syllables and the structure of words with the same general terms.

Every syllable contains a syllabic segment – usually a vowel – and most syllables have non-syllabic segments – consonants – before and after the syllabic segment. The syllabic element is the center, or **nucleus**, of the syllable. The consonant or consonants that precede the nucleus are the **onset** of the syllable, and the consonant or consonants that follow make up the **coda** of the syllable. The onset may be zero, as in the case of *end*, and there may be a zero coda, as in *plea*. The exclamation *Oh!* and the verb *owe*, both /ou/, have only a nucleus, with zero onset and zero coda. The structure of these seven syllables can be shown this way:

Onset	Nucleus	Coda
n	ɛ	d
d	ɛ	n
0	ɛ	nd
l	ii	p
p	ii	l
pl	ii	0
0	ou	0

Every syllable has a nucleus. There may be a zero onset or a zero coda, but there is no such thing as a zero nucleus.

Instead of saying that a syllable consists of onset, nucleus, and coda, we might instead say that a syllable consists of an onset and a

rhyme, and the rhyme consists of a nucleus and a coda. Then the structure of any syllable can be shown this way:

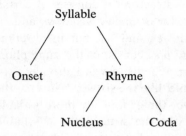

The reason for using the term 'rhyme' is fairly obvious: syllables that have the same nucleus and the same coda rhyme, as with *Ned–red–said–head* or *plea–see–free–knee*. However, there is a more subtle reason for recognizing a special relation between the nucleus and the coda. In English there are certain restrictions, or **constraints**, on what vowel, as nucleus, can be followed by what consonant(s) as coda. (Constraints like these are general in languages, but each language has its own constraints.)

There are likewise constraints on the occurrences of vowels. One particular constraint among vowels is seen in the distinction between **free vowels** and **checked vowels**. English has checked vowels like /ɛ/ and free vowels like /ii/. A checked vowel (V) must be followed by at least one consonant – there is no zero coda after a checked vowel, no English word pronounced, for example, /mɛ/ or /gæ/ or /lɪ/. A checked vowel can have a coda of one consonant (C), two consonants (CC), or three consonants (CCC), thus:

VC	chick, step, bat, good, rug, job
VCC	limp, chest, fact, wolf, pulse, fond
VCCC	jinx, tempt

A coda of three consonants is not common, and no English word ends with more than three consonant phonemes – unless it has a one-consonant inflection of the type surveyed in Section 6.3. The past tense of *jinx* is *jinxed* /jiŋkst/ and the third-person singular present tense of *tempt* is *tempts* /tɛmpts/, each ending with four consonants. However, this happens only when a suffix with the phoneme /t/ or /d/, /s/ or /z/, or /θ/ is added to other consonants, as in *jinx-ed* /jɪŋkst/, *tempt-s* /tɛmpts/.

A free vowel like /ii/ may have no consonant following, or one consonant or two, thus:

V   plea, day, brew, toe, tie, toy, now, spa, law
VC   sleep, bait, rude, yoke, life, voice, mouth, dawn
VCC   feast, saint, wound, coax, mild, point, lounge,

Codas of two consonants after a free vowel are rather special; the two consonants must be clusters like the ones illustrated: /st/, /nd/, /ld/, /nǰ/, and a few others. We will see more examples of constraints later in this chapter. Note that if a free vowel is followed by three consonants, it can only be in words like *feasts* /fiists/ and *lounged* /launǰd/, where the last consonant is a suffix.

If we consider every consonant (C) as one unit, every checked vowel (V) as one unit, and every free vowel (VV) as two units, then the rhyme of an English monosyllabic word (with no suffix) contains two to four units:

VC   VV   2
VCC   VVC   3
VCCC   VVCC   4

An English word may begin with no consonant (e.g. *ice*), one consonant (*rice*), two consonants (*spice*), or three consonants (*splice*) but no more. Putting this in a slightly different way, the onset of a syllable may be from zero to three consonants. Not just any two or any three consonants can occur in the onset; we have /tr/ as in *train* and /str/ as in *strain*, but no English word begins with /rt/ or /tsr/, for example. The constraints on consonant clusters in the onset and in the coda are examined in the next sections of this chapter.

At this point we should summarize the information of the past paragraphs with a more complete formula for the structure of an English syllable – more specifically, a monosyllabic word with no suffix. Any English word has an onset of from zero to three consonants and a rhyme which may be a checked vowel followed by from one to three consonants or a free vowel followed by from zero to two consonants. In the formula below, a superscript number indicates the maximum number, and the subscript number the minimum number, of possible consonants in a position.

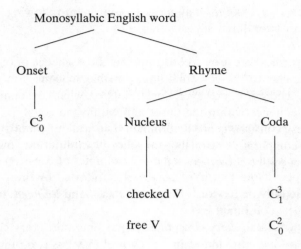

Divide these words into onset and rhyme, and rhyme into nucleus and coda, using our phonemic transcription:

dwarf grasp joke plank screw traipse

6.2 Consonants in clusters

Any single consonant can occur as the onset of an English word except /ŋ/ and /ʒ/. One example of each consonant in initial position follows.

pay bay toe dough chest jest cane gain
fan van thin then sue zoo shoe
mine nine lay ray yell well hell

A consonant or consonant cluster that occurs in the onset, such as /b/ or /tr/ or /str/ can generally be followed by any vowel, for example:

bend band bind boom beam bounce bone

train trend trim tree truce try trump
strain street strict stretch strap stripe

In other words, there are no constraints on the sequence of onset and nucleus similar to the constraints on possible sequences in nucleus and coda. There are, however, constraints on what consonants may occur in sequence within the onset and within the coda. To a large extent these constraints are determined by a scale of sonority.

The comparative resonance, or sonority, of different vowels and consonants can be shown this way:

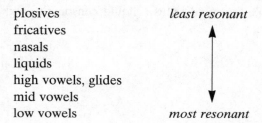

plosives   *least resonant*
fricatives
nasals
liquids
high vowels, glides
mid vowels
low vowels   *most resonant*

Very simply, there is greatest sonority in speech when the mouth is open widest and particles of air are vibrating in a large area in response to vibration of the vocal cords. There is least sonority when the oral and nasal cavities are completely closed. So lower vowels are more sonorant than higher vowels, which are more sonorant than sonorant consonants, which in turn are more sonorant than fricatives, and these outrank plosives in sonority.

When two consonants occur in the onset of a word, they follow the scale of sonority: an obstruent (plosive or fricative) may be followed by a sonorant consonant (liquid or glide) and a nasal consonant may be followed by a glide:

Cr-   pride, bride, train, drain, crease, grease, frill, thrill, shrill
Cl-   please, bleed, class, glass, flee
Cw-   twin, dwell, queen, thwart, whip
Cj-   pure, feud, cube, muse, new

but the reverse sequences are impossible.

Somewhat different from these sequences of obstruent + sonorant are the sequences of two glides, the glottal glide /h/ followed by /w/, as in *what, where, white* and /j/, as in *hew, huge, human*. The sequence /hw/ does not exist in many dialects, including RP, and is probably declining in other dialects, as it is replaced by /w/ alone, so that there is no contrast between *which* and *witch*, for instance.

The onset may consist of /s/ followed by another consonant, specifically /p t k f m n l w/:

sC-   spy, sty, sky, sphere, smile, snow, sleep, sweet

The sequences /sp st sk/ in the onset are exceptions to the rule of sonority; the more sonorant fricative /s/ precedes the less sonorant voiceless plosives.

A sequence of three consonants in the onset consists always of /s/ plus a voiceless plosive /p t k/ plus a liquid consonant or glide; expressed in a formula:

$$s \left\{ \begin{array}{c} p \\ t \\ k \end{array} \right\} \left\{ \begin{array}{c} l \\ r \\ w \\ j \end{array} \right\}$$

split spry spew street stew scream square

Possible kinds of consonant sequences are illustrated in Exhibit 6.1.

Now let's consider consonants in the coda. Any single consonant except /j w h/ may occur as coda of a syllable or word:

tap tab pat pad etch edge tack tag
leaf leave loath loathe rice rise push rouge
rum run rung bell bear

Sequences of two or three consonants roughly follow the scale of sonority; consequently the sequences are the opposite of onset clusters: the more sonorant consonants occur on the inside, next to the vowel and the less sonorant on the outside. Thus /r/ is followed by /l/ (but not the reverse): *curl*; either of them may be followed by a nasal: *elm*, *fern*; and a liquid or nasal can be followed by an obstruent:

sharp verb part card starch large stork berg
wharf carve birth force harsh
help bulb felt child mulch bulge silk
shelf shelve filth pulse Welsh
lamp ant hand lunch sponge bank
nymph month rinse lens

When two obstruents occur as a coda, they are both voiceless and they always include either /s/ or /t/ or both:

> lisp list risk lapse box adze apt act

A sequence of three consonants must consist of a liquid or a nasal plus two voiceless obstruents (always including /s/ or /t/):

> corpse quartz
> prompt distinct glimpse jinx against amongst

Clusters of three obstruents occur but are less common: *text*, *midst*.

═══════════════════ **EXHIBIT 6.1** Examples of consonant clusters in the onset

The symbol # marks syllable (or word) beginning.

Example	#	s	Obstruent	Nasal Liquid	Glide	Vowel
pray			p	r		ei
glow			g	l		ou
sleep		s		l		ii
muse				m	j	uu
stand		s	t			æ
try			t	r		ai
strive		s	t	r		ai
quit			k		w	ɪ
squint		s	k		w	ɪ
splurge		s	p	l		ɜ
			Glide		Glide	
wheat			h		w	ii
huge			h		j	uu

Note that this is a table of constraints. It does not specify the clusters that can occur; it specifies the limitations on what occurs. 'Nasal' and 'liquid' are mutually exclusive, for instance. The table has four positions but a cluster can be no more than three consonants.

═══

Exhibit 6.2 shows the general scheme for sequences of consonants in the coda (here # is at the right side and indicates the end of
syllable or word).

Among medial consonant clusters are some that also occur in
initial position:

whisper master whiskey
April citrus sacred
problem ticklish ugly

Other consonant clusters between vowels consist of a consonant
or consonant cluster that can occur in word-final position plus a
consonant or cluster that occurs word-initially:

mur.der sel.dom nap.kin ac.tor can.dy tem.per
bel.fry coun.try pil.grim ant.ler emp.ty
in.stant par.sley in.struct ob.struent

Since there can be as many as three consonants in final position and
three in initial position, there might, in theory, be medial clusters of
six consonants. In fact, there are no more than four consonants
between vowels in a simple (non-compound) English word.

instrument obstruct express /ɪksprés/ exclaim /ɪkskléim/

EXHIBIT 6.2 Examples of consonant clusters in the coda ━━━━━━━━

The symbol # here represents the word end.

Vowel	r	l	Nasal	Obstruent	s	t	#	Example
a	r			p				sharp
ɜ	r	l						curl
ɔ	r		n					horn
ɛ		l		f				shelf
ɪ				f		t		lift
ɒ				k	s			fox
ɪ		l	m					film
æ			ŋ	k				bank
æ				k		t		tact
æ				p	s			lapse

ɛ			k	s	t	next
ɛ		m	p		t	tempt
ɔ	r		p	s		corpse
ɪ		ŋ	k	s		lynx
ɜ	r	l	d			world

1 Think of two or more words (not necessarily one-syllable words) that begin with each of these consonant clusters. One example is given for the first.

spr-   sprint
sl-
ʃr
θr-
tw-
fl-
skw-

Think of two or more words that end with each of these consonant clusters.

-lθ
-nd
-nǰ
-sk
-ks
-ps
-lfθ   (There is only one word.)

2 This section has dealt chiefly with constraints on sequences of consonants in initial, medial, and final positions. There are also constraints on the occurrence of nucleus and coda – what vowels can be followed by what consonants. For example, /oi/ can occur with a zero coda (e.g. *joy*) or a coda with one or two tongue-tip consonants (e.g. *void, voice, noise,*

95

coin, *boil*, *point*, *moist*), but English has no words that end with /oip/, /oib/, /oič/, /oiǰ/, /oik/, or /oig/, for instance; only apical consonants occur after /oi/.

Which of the consonants and consonant clusters below occur as coda after /ai/? Think of a word that ends in /aip/, like *pipe*, and so on. If you can't think of a word fairly fast, there probably is no such sequence. When you finish, try to make a general statement about the constraints.

-p -b -t -d -č -ǰ -k -g
-f -v -s -z -ʃ -m -n -ŋ -l
-mp -nt -nd -sp -st -sk -lb -ld -lg

Which of these consonants and clusters occur after /au/? What constraints do you find?

6.3 Inflections

Some suffixes derive new words from the words to which they are attached; the suffix *-ful* makes an adjective *useful* from the noun *use*; the suffix *-ness* forms a noun like *usefulness*. An inflectional suffix, like the ones studied in this section, adds a grammatical meaning to the word to which it is attached. Here we take up four inflectional suffixes:

the regular plural suffix in nouns, like *horses*;
the possessive suffix in nouns, like *president's*;
the so-called third-person singular present in verbs, like (*he*) *kisses*;
the regular past tense suffix in verbs, like *kissed*.

The suffix which forms the plural number of regular nouns, written -(*e*)*s*, is pronounced /s/ or /z/ or /ɪz/ (alternatively, /əz/), depending on the last phoneme of the noun to which the suffix is added. Thus *cats* ends with /s/, *dogs* with /z/, and *horses* with /ɪz/. These three endings express the same meaning, plural number. Some morphemes – in fact, most morphemes – are always expressed the same way; other morphemes have two or more forms, called **allomorphs**. /s/, /z/ and /ɪz/ are regular allomorphs of the morpheme Plural, which also has irregular allomorphs, as in *oxen* and *children*.

These three allomorphs are regular because the choice of /s/ or /z/ or /ɪz/ depends on the last phoneme of the noun that is made plural. Again, the rule is known to every speaker of English but not necessarily with full awareness. The next exercise will help you figure out what the rule is.

EXERCISE 6.3

The nouns below illustrate all consonants and some vowels in word-final position. Write /s/, /z/, or /ɪz/ after each noun according to the pronunciation of the suffix, and then determine the rule that tells which allophone occurs after which phonemes.

club	lip	cuff	valve
bed	hat	smith	lathe
bridge	match	face	rose
egg	book	bush	garage
arm	can	ring	bell
tree	day	toe	car

Rule

(a) The regular plural suffix is pronounced /ɪz/ after
_____ ;
(b) it is pronounced /s/ after _____ ;
(c) it is pronounced /z/ after all other phonemes.

The regular possessive suffix also has three allomorphs, /s/, /z/, and /ɪz/, as in *Frank's*, *Joe's*, and *Rose's*. This is a different morpheme, 'possessive,' with the same allomorphs as the regular allomorphs of the morpheme 'plural.' Again, there is a rule that determines which allomorph occurs after what final phonemes.

EXERCISE 6.4

1 Add the possessive suffix to each of the following nouns and note where the suffix is pronounced /s/, where /z/, and where /ɪz/. How does the choice among these three depend on the last phoneme of the noun?

Chris Louise Mrs Fish Mr Birch   the judge
Hope Robert Dick Ralph Beth
Bob Ted Peg Steve Tom Ann Sue Joe Mary

Is the rule the same as for the regular plural morpheme?

2 Another suffix is the so-called 'third-person singular present' of verbs, as in (*she*) *likes*, (*it*) *moves*, (*he*) *wishes*, with the same three variants, /s z ɪz/. Examine the verbs below and determine the pronunciation of the suffix after each one. Is the rule the same as for the regular plural of nouns?

step	wait	reach	look
rub	need	budge	hug
laugh	race	finish	hum
love	breathe	raise	massage
fan	play	annoy	gnaw

The suffix -*ed*, which forms the past tense of a regular verb has three different pronunciations, /t/, /d/, and /ɪd/ (or /əd/); for example *looked* is /lʊkt/, *begged* is /bɛgd/, and *waited* is /wéitɪd/. These three endings express the same meaning, 'past tense,' therefore they express the same morpheme. /t/, /d/, and /ɪd/ are three allomorphs of the morpheme 'past tense,' and there are other allomorphs seen in irregular verbs.

Why are these three allomorphs 'regular'? Because the choice of /t/ or /d/ or /ɪd/ depends on the last phoneme of the verb to which the suffix is added. There is a rule which all speakers of English know – though they aren't necessarily aware that they know it – and which determines whether we add /t/ or /d/ or /ɪd/ to the pronunciation of a regular verb.

Examine the data in the next exercise and figure out what the rule is.

The verbs listed below illustrate all the consonants and some vowels in word-final position. Write /t/, /d/, or /ɪd/ after each verb according to the pronunciation of the suffix. Then figure out the rule which determines the pronunciation.

hope	lift	touch	cook
rub	need	budge	hug
laugh	kiss	wish	aim
live	breathe	choose	massage
fan	long	tie	flow

Rule

(a) The regular past tense is pronounced /ɪd/ after verbs that end with ___ or ___ ;

(b) it is pronounced /t/ after _____;

(c) it is pronounced /d/ after all other phonemes.

LOOKING BACK

Every syllable has a peak or nucleus. Consonants that precede the nucleus constitute the onset of the syllable; consonants that follow make up the coda of the syllable. Nucleus and coda together are the rhyme. Every language has constraints regarding what consonants and vowels may occur in sequence. Statements about what sequences of phonemes are possible and what sequences are impossible in a language constitute the phonotactics of that language. In learning a foreign language, acquiring the pronunciation of new kinds of sequences may present a challenge.

In part, sequences of consonants follow a scale of sonority. The word *print* illustrates something close to a norm for a mono-syllabic word with a two-consonant onset and a two-consonant coda:

Obstruent C – Sonorant C – Vowel – Sonorant C – Obstruent C

If, instead of obstruent consonant + sonorant consonant, two obstruents occur in the onset, the first must be /s/; if two obstruents occur in the coda, they are voiceless and include /s/ or /t/ or both. If three consonants occur in the onset, the first is /s/, the second /p/, /t/, or /k/, the third /r/, /l/, /w/, or /j/. Three consonants in the coda are mostly sonorant consonant plus two obstruent consonants, again with the constraint that the obstruents are voiceless and include /s/ and/or /t/. Intervocalic consonant clusters are of the same types as occur word-initially or they are sequences of consonants that occur in word-final position plus consonants that occur in initial position.

There are likewise constraints on the occurrence of vowels. One particular constraint among vowels is seen in the distinction between free vowels and checked vowels. The former occur in word-final position and when followed by single consonants and a very small number of possible consonant clusters. The latter do not occur finally but can be followed by single consonants and consonant clusters.

Other constraints are seen in certain common inflectional suffixes. There are three morphemes, Plural number, Possessive, and Third Person Singular Present, which are expressed in the same way. Each of these morphemes has the same three allomorphs, all containing a sibilant consonant. After a word that ends with a sibilant consonant, the allomorph is /-iz/ because English does not permit two sibilants together in word-final position. After a word that ends with any other voiceless consonant, the allomorph is /-s/; English requires two final obstruents to agree in voicing. When the last phoneme of the word is neither sibilant nor voiceless, the allomorph is /-z/. Another inflectional morpheme, Past Tense, has three regular allomorphs also. The allomorph /-id/ occurs after /t/ and /d/ (it would be impossible for a word to end with /tt/ or /dd/). The allomorph /t/ occurs after other voiceless consonants, and the allomorph /d/ in all other places.

Suggested readings

Roach (1990: Chapter 8) is an alternative description of the syllable in English. See Ladefoged (1993: Chapter 10) for a treatment of prosodic phenomena associated with syllables in numerous languages.

Chapter 7

Strong and weak syllables

- **7.1 Accent and stress** 102
- **7.2 Weak syllables** 109
- **7.3 Variation in weak syllables** 112

LOOKING AHEAD

When we speak, we use more energy in producing some syllables than others and, when we listen to other people speaking, we recognize that some parts of a speaker's utterances are more prominent than others: the syllables are generally louder, longer, and different in pitch from the surrounding syllables. To explain – and understand – these facts we need to recognize a difference between **accent** and **stress**, and we need to recognize a distinction between **strong** syllables and **weak** syllables. (See Section 7.1.)

The nucleus of a strong syllable is one of the vowels that occur in monosyllabic words, surveyed in Chapter 5. The nucleus of a weak syllable is more variable, more likely to be a schwa or a syllabic consonant. (See Section 7.2.)

Different styles of speaking depend very much on the individual and on the formality or informality of the speech situation. We speak faster or slower, less or more carefully depending on where we are, what kind of things we have to say, and to whom we are talking. However, there are general tendencies that apply to the English language as a whole. In English utterances, stressed syllables of lexical words are strong and long, while unstressed syllables are weak and short. These syllables do not change, but some common function words show variation between strong forms and weak forms. The weak forms are due to four phonetic processes: **vowel reduction**, **vowel loss**, **consonant loss**, and **assimilation**. A special kind of assimilation is **palatalization**. (See Section 7.3.)

7.1 Accent and stress

Some utterances consist of a single word with a single syllable, e.g. *Yes*, *No*, *Right*. That syllable, since it constitutes a whole utterance, must have an intonation. The voice may fall, as in giving an answer

(↓*Yes.*), or rise, as in asking for confirmation (↑*Yes?*). The topic of intonation is studied in detail in Chapter 10. Here we use just two symbols, the upward arrow, ↑, and downward arrow, ↓, for rising and falling intonation, respectively. We also write the question mark and period as they are used conventionally, but we need to note that conventional punctuation does not represent intonation accurately or consistently.

Most utterances, of course, consist of several words and therefore of several syllables.

Tóm bóught twó néw ↓bóoks.

In this utterance the words are almost equally loud and equally long, so that the utterance has a sort of staccato rhythm, but the last word is slightly longer and more prominent because it has the accent of the utterance. Each word is stressed and the last word is accented.

The staccato rhythm, or syllabic timing, in this utterance is due to the fact that each word is a monosyllable and also a lexical word. Such utterances are not normal for English. Most English utterances contain short, weak syllables – because the lexical words consist of more than one syllable, as in:

Thómas púrchased twénty remárkable récords.

or because the utterance contains function words, which are typically weak, as in:

Tóm was búying a númber of ↓bóoks.

Unstressed syllables are weak and occupy less time than stressed syllables.

Some short phrases and sentences are composed only of lexical words, like these:

a noun phrase

number + noun	fóur ↓dáys
adjective + noun	níce ↓gírl
first name + family name	Chrís ↑Brówn?

a verb phrase

verb + noun	séll ↑ríce?
verb + adverb	stáy ↓hére

a whole sentence

noun + verb	Ánn ↓léft.

In contrast, the phrases and sentences below do not have equal stress. One word, a function word, is unstressed; the other, a lexical word, is stressed, as well as accented.

a noun phrase

article (*a*, *the*) + noun	the ↓bóys
possessive pronoun + noun	my ↓tíes
title (*Miss*, *Mister*) + noun	Miss ↓Brówn

a prepositional phrase

preposition + noun	by ↑pláne?

a sentence

pronoun + verb	She ↓léft.
verb + pronoun	↓Táke it.

Every word of more than one syllable has one stressed syllable. The position of stress in the word is fixed: *ánimal*, *tomórrow*, *indepéndent*, and *recommendátion* are stressed, respectively, on the first, second, third, and fourth syllables. Speakers of English are not free to stress whatever syllable they want. However, over time the position of stress has changed in some words, and sometimes the changes have occurred in some dialects but not others. Exhibit 7.1 is a list of some common words that are stressed differently by different speakers of the language.

━━━━━━━━━━━━━━━━━━━━━━━━━━ **EXHIBIT 7.1** Some words stressed differently

Words borrowed from Modern French are generally stressed on the initial syllable in British English but on the final syllable in American English. Examples:

> ballet baton café caffeine cliché crochet frontier garage

But *camouflage* is stressed on the first syllable and *champagne* on the last syllable by all speakers.

Two-syllable verbs that end with the suffix *-ate*, like the following, are stressed on the last syllable in British English:

> create dictate migrate narrate rotate vibrate

All but the first of these are stressed on the first syllable in American English. (This does not include verbs that begin with a prefix, like *debate* and *inflate*.)

━━

While the stress of a word is essentially fixed, the accent of a tone unit can be placed on any word – that is, on the stressed syllable of any word.

> Tóm bóught ↓tén néw bóoks. (emphasizing the number)
> ↓Tóm bóught tén néw bóoks. (emphasizing the buyer)

Mobile accent – the possible occurrence of accent on any word in a tone unit – is characteristic of English and other Germanic languages, a characteristic that is by no means found in all languages. By accenting different words in what would otherwise be the same utterance a speaker creates differences of focus, which are subtle differences of meaning. Chapter 10 discusses these semantic differences.

Although function words are ordinarily unstressed and weak (like *a* or *the*), any word can be accented, and then it becomes strong. (In fact, this is the best way to define a word in English: a word is any part of the vocabulary that can be the accented item in a tone unit.)

> I háve ↓á /ei/ péncil.   (just one pencil, not more)
> ↓thé /ðii/ Sálly Dávidson   (of all people who may have this name, the one who is famous)
> góvernment ↓óf the péople

Let's examine the matter of weak and strong unstressed syllables in words and in phrases:

separate (adjective)	/sɛpərət/
separate (verb)	/sɛpəreit/
difficulty (British)	/dífikəlti/
difficulty (American)	/dífikʌlti/
multiplication	/mʌltiplikéiʃən/
elimination	/ilɪminéiʃən/
They waited for us.	/ðei ↓wéitid fɔr əs/
They waited for us	/ðei ↓wéitid fər ʌs/

The written word *separate* corresponds to two different spoken words, an adjective and a verb. Both words are pronounced with an initial stressed syllable followed by two unstressed syllables. In the adjective the last syllable is weak, with the vowel /ə/; the last syllable of the verb is strong, with the vowel /ei/. (There are a number of written words like this, each representing two or more words that belong to different parts of speech and have different pronunciations. Exhibit 7.2 contains several examples.) So long as we write such words in phonemic transcription, the difference is obvious, but it is often convenient, in a book like this one, to use the conventional orthography, in which case we need some special way of distinguishing a strong unstressed syllable (like /-reit/) from a weak unstressed syllable (like /-rət/). We use the symbol ` over the vowel letter (or first vowel letter) of a strong unstressed syllable; a weak unstressed syllable gets no mark; thus, *séparàte* (verb), *séparate* (adjective).

EXHIBIT 7.2 One written word = two or more spoken words ▬▬▬▬▬

Verb /-eit/	Adjective /-ət/	Noun /-ət/
advocate		advocate
affiliate		affiliate
alternate	alternate	alternate
appropriate	appropriate	
delegate		delegate
duplicate	duplicate	duplicate
elaborate	elaborate	
estimate		estimate
graduate		graduate
intimate	intimate	
moderate	moderate	

predicate		predicate
separate	separate	
subordinate	subordinate	subordinate

Verb /-mɛnt/	*Noun* /-mənt/
compliment	compliment
experiment	experiment
implement	implement
ornament	ornament
supplement	supplement

EXHIBIT 7.3 Words with weak or strong penult, like *difficulty*

British		*North American*	
Jánuary	/ǰænju(ə)ri/	Jánuàry	/ǰænjuèri/
líbrary	/láibr(ər)i/	líbràry	/láibrèri/
líterary	/lítər(ər)i/	líteràry	/lítərèri/
sécretary	/sékrət(ə)ri/	sécretàry	/sékrətèri/
vocábulary	/vəkǽbjələri/	vocábulàry	/vokǽbjulèri/
dórmitory	/dɔ́rmit(ə)ri/	dórmitòry	/dɔ́rmitòri/
térritory	/térit(ə)ri/	térritòry	/téritòri/
céremony	/sérəməni/	céremòny	/sérəmòni/
mátrimony	/mǽtriməni/	mátrimòny	/mǽtrimòni/

However, for *necessary*, /nésɪsèri/ seems to be about as common in Britain as /nésɪsri/, and in North America *interesting* is at least as likely to be pronounced /íntrɪstɪŋ/ as /íntərèstɪŋ/.

Finally, we need to recognize that prepositions, pronouns, and other function words, while typically unstressed, may be strong or weak. In the sentence "They waited for us," for example, *for* and *us* are both likely to be unstressed. However, either one can be strong and the other weak. The phonemic transcriptions above make this clear because they show different vowel symbols. For convenience, we can also show the difference this way:

Thèy ↓wáited for ùs.
Thèy ↓wáited fòr us.

Any word can be accented (but not any strong syllable).

To review a bit, let's notice four kinds of syllables in this utterance:

Sálly àdvísed ùs to wáit fòr the néxt ↓tráin.

Here *train* is the most prominent syllable, the accented syllable. It is strong and long and pronounced with a change of pitch, in this case with falling pitch. As noted previously, we can produce different utterances with the same sequence of words by putting the accent on a different word, for example, on *next* or *wait* or *us*.

PRACTICE 7.1

Read the following sentences aloud with a falling intonation in the way you would 'normally' speak them. Then mark the accented syllable (↓) and every stressed syllable (´) in each sentence. Use the grave diacritic (`) to mark every strong unstressed syllable.

(a) We invited them over for drinks.
(b) Alison spent three years at Stanford.
(c) I can manage this job by myself.
(d) Rudy received a message from Judy.
(e) Little Bo-Peep has lost her sheep.
(f) Rome wasn't built in a day.
(g) Don't count your chickens before they're hatched.
(h) Don't cross the bridge before you come to it.
(i) Please turn down the thermostat.
(j) Business is fairly good now.

A function word often becomes attached to a lexical word and the two together form a single phonological word: *take it* is one phonological word like *ticket*; the phrase *for giving* is like the word *forgiving*.

7.2 Weak syllables

The vowel which is the nucleus of a strong syllable can always be identified with one of the key words introduced in Chapter 4: the second syllable of *command* has the vowel of SPA or of BAT, depending on where the speaker comes from; the first syllable of *soda* has the vowel of TOE, the middle syllable of *develop* has the vowel of STEP; and so on.

Identifying the nucleus of a weak syllable is more troublesome. Do the words *develop*, *preventable*, and *evacuation* have the same vowel in the first syllable? And if so, is it to be equated with TREE or CHICK or something else? The same question can be asked about the vowel in the second syllable of *radium* and the vowel in the last syllable of *originality*. How about the second syllable of *virtue* and the third syllable of *evacuation*? Is that the vowel of TRUE or of FOOT? Different speakers of English give different answers to all these questions. The point is that weak syllables do not have as many contrasting vowel phonemes as strong syllables and so, where contrast is less important, there is more variation in what is pronounced.

The most common unstressed vowel is the mid-central /ə/, called schwa. It occurs in the first and last syllables of *arena*, for example, and in the syllables of these words, where the vowel letter is italicized:

> c*o*mm*a*nd sod*a* devel*o*p capit*a*l radi*u*m
> prevent*a*ble *o*riginality

The unstressed vowel at the end of *happy*, *easy*, *policy* and the like and the pre-vocalic vowel of *radium*, *furious*, *maniac* may be equated with /ii/, the vowel of TREE, or /ɪ/, the vowel of CHICK. In terms of pronunciation it is either of them; in regard to the system of phonemes it is neither of them because there is no contrast – the contrast between these high front, strong-syllable vowels is neutralized in weak syllables. We use the symbol /i/ to represent it – something varying between /ii/ and /ɪ/.

Similarly, the weak final vowel of *value*, *issue*, *menu* and the pre-vocalic vowel of *casual*, *virtuous*, *evacuate* is either /uu/ as in TRUE or /ʊ/ as in FOOT, or it is neither of them. We use a symbol /u/ for the neutralization of these high back, strong-syllable vowels in weak syllables. In the following, where the vowel letter is italicized, do you pronounce a high front /i/ or mid central /ə/?

develop prevent evacuate capital modification

In the next group, does the italicized vowel letter stand for the high back /u/ or for /ə/ in your usual pronunciation?

July prudential accurate masculine popular

Some speakers have a weak vowel /o/ in some or all of the following:

obey Korea accolade potato yellow

Others are likely to have /ə/ in the first three and /ou/ in the last two.

In non-rhotic dialects the following words have /ə/ in the second syllable:

better cover commerce drunkard western

and in the first syllable of these:

curtail pertain surpass verbatim

In rhotic dialects what is pronounced is a schwa with R-coloring, that is, a vowel sound like /ə/ but with the tongue drawn back slghtly and with a groove in the tongue-tip. The IPA symbol is [ɚ]. Alternatively, this may be interpreted as the sonorant consonant /r/ occurring as the nucleus of a syllable, [r̩]. In *mirror, terror, horror*, for instance, there is a non-syllabic /r/ followed by a syllabic /r̩/. In rapid speech the two sometimes blend into a single prolonged /r:/: [mɪr:], for example.

Syllabic /l/, [l̩], occurs in weak syllables, especially after the apical consonants /t d s z/ as in these examples:

metal fiddle muscle puzzle catalogue
battle candle castle easel What'll we do?

The tongue-tip is in position for the apical consonant and the tongue-back for a dark /l/, which follows immediately without an intervening vowel. After non-apical consonants syllabic /l/ is possible or there may be a schwa before /l/ is articulated.

couple level satchel tackle wiggle

Syllabic /n/, [n̩], is frequent in weak syllables after apical and laminal obstruents /t d s z č ǰ ʃ ʒ/.

Britain sudden lesson reason
question pigeon fashion vision
doesn't hadn't present patient
monotony fascinate passionate

In rapid speech syllabic /n/ can occur after other obstruents, for example in *open* or *taken*. In fact, *open* may have a syllabic [m̩] and *taken* a syllabic [ŋ̩].

PRACTICE 7.2

Some speakers have /ə/ in the final, weak syllables of *ballot* and *human*, /i/ in the weak syllables of *ticket* and *chicken*; other speakers make no such distinction. Examine your pronunciation of the weak syllables in the following. Do you have /ə/ in some and /i/ in others? If so, do both occur before the same consonant, as in *ballot* and *ticket*, *human* and *chicken*? Or does /ə/ occur before some consonants, /i/ before others?

olive cherub gallop Philip bucket palate ceiling polish
orange sandwich palace Alice hammock comic solid salad
advantage rushes Russia's

Function words typically occur in a phrase with one or more lexical words:

determiner + noun	the table, some food, any money
auxiliary + verb	are working, have gone, can tell
preposition + noun phrase	of coffee, for money, at pictures
pronoun + verb	he is, she has, it will
verb + pronoun	see him, tell her, take it, use them

Function words also occur together:

preposition + pronoun   with it, about her, for them
auxiliary + auxiliary   should have, must be, has been

7.3 Variation in weak syllables

Each utterance below has a function word that occurs twice.

Mr Brówn is léaving now I but I dón't thínk his wífe is.
Páula has réad the assígnment I but I dóubt if Súsan has.
Gáry can stáy anóther hóur. I Do you suppóse wé can?
Ánn will be áble to atténd the pláy I and máybe Ándy will.
I'd líke to sée the Taj Mahál I sóme dáy I but I dón't expéct to.

In the first tone unit of each utterance the function words (*is*, *has*, *can*, *will*, *to*) are in a weak position, between stressed words, and they can be weakened still further with reduction of the vowel – /tuu/ becomes /tə/, for instance; loss of the vowel – /ɪz/ becomes /z/; even loss of the initial consonant and vowel – /hæz/ becomes just /z/. These are all kinds of phonetic weakening. The same function words are also in utterance-final position in these examples, where they are strong, though unstressed, and cannot be weakened phonetically. In utterance-initial position ("Is Mr Brówn léaving?" and the like) phonetic weakening is less likely than in the interior of the utterance and any reduction that happens will be due to rapidity of speech. Of course, when a function word is accented ("Mr Brown ↓ís going"), it is strong and not reducible.

Phonetic weakening is a kind of simplification, reduction of the efforts that have to be made to pronounce a sequence of phonemes. Phonetic weakening occurs in weak syllables – the weak syllables of lexical words and function words when these are in weak position – and it includes four processes: vowel reduction, consonant loss, vowel loss, and assimilation.

Vowel reduction

It apparently takes less effort to pronounce a central vowel, like /ə/, than to move the tongue to a forward or back position. A vowel, especially a checked vowel, is reduced to /ə/ – and the sequence of /ə/

plus a sonorant consonant may be realized as a syllabic consonant. For example, pronounced in isolation or with emphasis the words *a*, *an*, *the* and *some* are, respectively, /ei/, /æn/, /ðii/, and /sʌm/. When they occur before a noun, they are usually unstressed and their respective pronunciations are /ə/, /ən/, /ðə/ before a consonant and /ði/ before a vowel, /səm/. Other examples of such vowel reduction appear in Exhibit 7.4.

EXHIBIT 7.4 Some examples of vowel reduction

In the initial syllable of lexical words:

/æ/ or /ə/ abstain, accelerate, admit, Atlantic
/i/ or /ə/ because, decide, prepare, receive
/ɛ/ or /ɪ/ eccentric, employ, example, except
/o/ or /ə/ occasion, opinion, potential, produce

In function words:

Do you need any help?	/ɛni/	> /əni/, [n̩i]
We might as well.	/æz/	> /əz/
Look at that clown.	/æt/	> /ət/
You can do it.	/kæn/	> /kən/, [kn̩]
This is for you.	/fɔ(r)/	> /fə(r)/
a week or so	/ɔ(r)/	> /ə(r)/
You should be careful.	/ʃʊd/	> /ʃəd/

Just as *the* has one reduced form before words that begin with a vowel and another before consonant-initial words, *do*, *to*, and *you* have a change of /uu/ to /ə/ before consonants and to /u/ before vowels. (Some speakers have /ə/ even before vowels.)

How do you get there? /dəjə/
I'd like to see it. /tə/

Consonant loss

Not producing a consonant is simpler than producing one. Clusters of consonants are likely to be reduced within lexical words; for example, in *Arctic* the cluster /-(r)kt-/ often loses the /k/; similarly, the /g/ of *English* is omitted and so is the /d/ of *sandwich*. Consonant clusters formed where words come together undergo the same kind of reduction; *the next train*, from our example sentence in Section 7.1, loses the first /t/ of the sequence / . . . kst tr . . . /; *second chance* is likely to be spoken without a /d/. The following examples concern function words in weak positions.

Initial /h/ is lost in the pronouns *he, his, him, her* and in *have* when this is an auxiliary verb. There is also vowel reduction and final /v/ may be lost – more likely before a consonant than before a vowel.

How long did he work?	/ . . . dɪdi . . . /
He's worried about his exams.	/ . . . əbautɪz . . . /
I hope to meet her soon.	/ . . . miitə(r) . . . /
They must have had an accident.	/ . . . mʌstə(v) . . . /
You should have told us.	/ . . . ʃʊdə(v) . . . /

The pronoun *them* has a shortened form without initial consonant, though historically this reduced form is derived from a different Old English pronoun, *hem*.

Did you tell 'em?   / . . . tɛləm/

The sequence / . . . zð . . . / is frequent in speech: *is, was, has, does* + *the* or *there*. Omission of /ð/ often occurs:

Is the radio on?   /ɪzə . . . /

The initial consonant of *will, would* is lost, along with vowel reduction, but never at the begnning of a tone unit.

There'll probably be time enough. /ðɛrəl . . . /
That'd be wonderful.   /ðætəd . . . /

The /v/ of *of* is generally lost before a following consonant.

a cup of coffee   / . . . kʌpə . . . /

The final consonant of *must* may disappear before a following consonant.

You must put that off till later.   / ... məs pʊt ... /

The final consonant of *and* is also omitted but not only before a following consonant. In fact, the usual conversational pronunciation is /ən/, [ŋ̩]; /ænd/ is normal only in formal speech.

Vowel loss

Similarly, it is simpler to omit a vowel than to pronounce one, but not if omitting the vowel brings together consonants that require very different articulations. In words that have two weak syllables in the coda the first vowel is likely to be omitted in rapid speech, especially if the next consonant is /l/ or /r/: *family*, *history*, *camera*, etc.

Just as the contraction *I'm* results from loss of /æ/, so other contractions of personal pronouns with forms of *be*, *have*, *will*, and *would* show vowel loss along with initial consonant loss.

	I	*he*	*she*	*it*	*we*	*you*	*they*
am	I'm						
is		he's	she's	it's			
are					we're	you're	they're
have	I've				we've	you've	they've
has		he's	she's	it's			
had	I'd	he'd	she'd	it'd	we'd	you'd	they'd
will	I'll	he'll	she'll	it'll	we'll	you'll	they'll
would	I'd	he'd	she'd	it'd	we'd	you'd	they'd

The contractions with *has* are the same as the contractions with *is* and the contractions with *would* are like the contractions with *had*. Syntax usually differentiates them: *she's writing*, *she's written*, *we'd enjoyed it*, *we'd enjoy it*.

The vowel of *is*, /ɪz/ is reduced not only after pronouns but in practically any medial position. It becomes /ɪz/ or /əz/ after a sibilant consonant, /s/ after other voiceless consonants, /z/ in all other cases. Further, the auxiliary verb *has* loses its initial consonant as well as the vowel under the same conditions as *is*, and undergoes the same assimilation.

After sibilant consonants: /ɪz/ or /əz/

> Alice's busy.
> Rose's been busy.
> Mr Bush's retired.
> The judge's waiting.
> Miss Rich's been away lately.

After voiceless non-sibilant consonants: /s/

> Hope's here, Bert's here, Dick's here, Ralph's here.
> Mrs Smith's written another poem.

Elsewhere: /z/

> Bob's here, Ed's here, Meg's here, Steve's here.
> The baby's awake.
> Mr King's read the report.

You recognize that these reductions of *is* and *has* are identical with the regular allomorphs of the morpheme Plural, the morpheme Possessive, and the morpheme Third Person Singular of present tense verbs (Chapter 6).

Assimilation

It is generally easier to produce two consonants in sequence if they are alike in some feature(s) – voice, place of articulation, etc. – than to pronounce a sequence of consonants that differ considerably. Assimilation is making one phoneme more like another.

The change of /z/ to /s/ after other phonemes are deleted in *is* and *has*, is an example of one kind of **assimilation**; the final voiceless phoneme of the noun affects the following phoneme; a voiced consonant becomes voiceless. A change like this, in which a phoneme is affected by a preceding phoneme, is called 'regressive assimilation.' A more common kind of change is 'progressive (or anticipatory) assimilation,' in which one phoneme takes on some feature of a following phoneme. Exhibit 7.5 has examples of such progressive assimilation.

EXHIBIT 7.5 Progressive assimilation

1   In casual speech the final /n/ of *can, in, on* is likely to become
/m/ before a labial consonant and /ŋ/ before a dorsal consonant
– an assimilation in place of articulation.

You can buy it here.	/ . . . kəmbai . . . /
You can pay over there.	
It's in back.	
We can go later.	/ . . . kəŋgou . . . /
You can come with us.	
He's on guard.	

The apical nasal /n/ becomes assimilated to a labial or dorsal
consonant, as in the examples above, but /m/ and /ŋ/ do not
assimilate. For example, in *from door to door* /m/ does not
change, nor does /ŋ/ in *long time*.

2   The sequence /zʃ/ is rather frequent: *is she, does she, has she,
was she*. The first sibilant can change to /ʒ/: /ɪʒʃi/, and so on.
This is also a change in place of articulation. The change of /z/
to /ʒ/ and the change of /n/ to /m/ or /ŋ/ are instances of partial
assimilation. If *is she* is realized as /ɪʃʃi/, there is complete
assimilation. In *horseshoe* and *space ship* the sequence /sʃ/ is
likely to undergo complete assimilation.

3   Assimilation in voice occurs in *have to* /hæftuu/, *has to* /hæstuu/.
Note that this is not the auxiliary verb *have*; it does not undergo
consonant or vowel loss or reduction.

The contractions of pronouns with forms of *be, have, do,* and
other auxiliary verbs, listed above, are formed by processes – vowel
reduction, vowel loss, consonant loss – that are in effect in present-
day English. We see the same effects in other word constructions.
The contractions of the same verbs with *not*, shown in the chart
below, result from changes that happened in an earlier stage of
English.

Auxiliary verbs + *not*

am	–	can	can't
is	isn't	could	couldn't

are	aren't	will	won't
was	wasn't	would	wouldn't
were	weren't	shall	shan't
has	hasn't	should	shouldn't
have	haven't	may	–
had	hadn't	might	mightn't
does	doesn't	must	mustn't
do	don't	ought	oughtn't
did	didn't	need	needn't

Most of these forms have a syllabic /n/, which would result from loss of a vowel in *not*, but there is no other instance in present-day English of a syllabic consonant resulting from loss of a vowel after that consonant. The contractions *don't* and *won't* are obviously not derived from the present pronunciations of *do* and *will* + *not*. In *can't, shan't, don't,* and *won't* /n/ is not syllabic; /n/ is syllabic in some pronunciations of *aren't* and *weren't*, not syllabic in other pronunciations.

A special kind of mutual assimilation is **palatalization**, which occurs when the apical consonants /t d s z/ in word-final position come into contact with an initial /j/ in the following word. The sequences /t–j d–j s–j z–j/ become, respectively, /č ǰ ʃ ʒ/.

won't you	/wounčuu/
did you	/dɪǰuu/
unless you . . .	/ʌnlɛʃuu/
as you . . .	/æʒuu/
Would you like to come along?	/wuǰuu . . . /
not yet	/nɒčet/

Finally, we should note that not all function words undergo these phonological processes. The prepositions *by, down, in, off, on, out, through, up* do not have reduced forms, nor do two-syllable prepositions like *about* and *beside*. Auxiliary verbs with free vowels, like *may, might,* and *ought,* do not reduce, nor do the pronouns *she, we, me,* and *they*.

LOOKING BACK

Every tone unit has an accented syllable, which differs in pitch from other syllables. Accent indicates the most important or most informative word in the tone unit. Unaccented words may be stressed or not, depending on how much they contribute to the message; generally, content words are stressed and function words are not. An accented syllable is stressed, and every stressed syllable is strong. Some unstressed syllables are strong and others weak.

Strong syllables have strong vowels, the vowels that occur in monosyllabic words. In weak syllables the number of contrasting vowels is reduced. Some weak syllables have syllabic (sonorant) consonants: syllabic /n/ and /l/ are frequent and, in rhotic dialects, syllabic /r/; syllabic /m/ and /ŋ/ can be heard in fast or casual speech replacing /n/. Function words that undergo these processes do not lose their meanings nor change their meanings; all that changes is the pronunciation of the forms. The changes are not random or irregular. Particular vowels and consonants undergo particular changes in certain environments.

The processes include vowel reduction, vowel loss, consonant loss, and assimilation. The first three of these are different kinds of weakening. Assimilation is a replacement of one phoneme by another due to the influence of a neighboring phoneme. When the replacement is due to a following phoneme, the assimilation is regressive; in a progressive assimilation the replacing phoneme is more like some preceding phoneme than the phoneme replaced. One kind of mutual assimilation is palatalization.

Among fast forms are the so-called contractions, abbreviated forms of constructions: personal subject pronouns combined with forms of *be*, *have*, *do*, *will*, and *would*; and forms of *be*, *have*, *do*, *can*, *could*, *will*, *would*, *shall*, *should*, *must*, and *need* with *not*. Some of these can be seen as derived from the full constructions by the same processes of vowel reduction or vowel loss as in the function words discussed above. Other contractions reflect pronunciations of an earlier time.

Vowel weakening and vowel loss can be attributed to the stress timing that is characteristic of English. Stressed syllables are given more time (as well as force) than unstressed syllables, usually producing a rhythm of uneven beats. Some phoneticians have maintained that English utterances have a rhythm that is determined by the number of strong syllables. According to them, the phrases *bláck cáts*, *some yéllow kíttens*, and *the trúmpeting élephants*, for example, each get the same amount of time: there are two strong beats and any number of weak syllables are 'squeezed' into the same time period. While such a phenomenon may be true for some speakers of English, it seems dubious for all varieties of the language, since tempos and speech styles clearly vary from dialect to dialect.

Suggested reading

Roach (1991: Chapter 14) takes a different look at theories of English rhythm and how they affect the phonological processes discussed in this chapter.

Notes

1　Linguists have not generally agreed on the treatment of relative prominence in English – the number of relevant differences and how these should be interpreted and named. However, when allowances are made for variant terminology, something close to consensus appears. Jones (1977), for example, (usually referred to as *EPD*) recognizes three degrees of 'stress,' full stress (indicated by a raised tick, ', before the syllable), half stress (shown by a lowered tick, ,), and unstress (no mark). In addition, some compound words, like '*ill-*'*tempered*, have two full stresses, which may be further differentiated by a tone – a change of pitch – on the stressed syllable of *tempered* in, for example, *Johnny is rather ill-tempered today*, so that in fact four kinds of syllables are noted. Trager and Smith (1951), a work which was long influential among American linguists, insisted on the existence in English of four degrees of stress, quite apart from differences of pitch. Against this view, Gimson (1994 and earlier) maintained that what is called 'stress' is not a single thing but a number of physical facts that can make one syllable stand out from its neighboring syllables: different pitch, greater intensity, greater length, and difference of quality. Vanderslice and Ladefoged (1972; see also Ladefoged 1993, Chapter 5) resolved these facts into three binary features, accented/unaccented, stressed/unstressed, strong/weak (in their terminology, [+accent]/[–accent], [+stress]/[–stress], [+strong]/[–strong]. This is the model used here.

　　We use the acute and grave diacritics in this book, instead of raised and lowered ticks employed in some other works, for purely pragmatic reasons: the raised tick is easily confused with an apostrophe in most typefaces and in fact is identical with it in some.

2   In the language of every day, words often have a number of meanings, not all of them clearly distinguished. When scientists adopt an ordinary word as a technical term in their discipline, they seek to establish its use with a single, well-defined area of application. Unfortunately, scientists do not always agree on which of the common meanings should be the technical meaning. This is the case with the word *accent*. In everyday usage *accent* means (1) the way of speaking of a particular group of people ('a Scottish accent,' 'a foreign accent'); (2) emphasis given to a particular part, or parts, of an utterance and the prominence resulting from this emphasis (akin to the verb *accentuate*); (3) one of various diacritic marks ('acute,' 'grave,' 'circumflex,' etc.) used to augment the alphabet in different ways, including marks to indicate the prominence mentioned in definition (2). Though the first sense is necessarily somewhat vague, a lot of linguists use *accent just* this way, to indicate the pronunciation typical of some group within a larger language community. The most notable example is Wells (1982).

Accent is used here in a way closer to that of the second definition above. Accent is the change of pitch, or difference of pitch, that occurs on one syllable in a tone unit. A syllable with this pitch distinction is the accented syllable of the tone unit and, by extension, the word in which it occurs is the accented word. The term *sentence stress* has been used with something like the meaning intended here for 'accent,' but that usage would destroy the useful distinction between accent and stress, and the word 'sentence' is not appropriate since a tone unit does not necessarily coincide with a sentence.

Word stress

- **8.1 The phonological structure of words: stress patterns**   124

- **8.2 The morphological structure of words**   130

- **8.3 Rules for stress in simple words**   135

LOOKING AHEAD

In every word of two or more syllables one syllable is stressed, for example, the middle syllable of *remember*. We describe the structure of a word with the same terms that we used for describing the parts of a syllable – onset, nucleus, and coda. Here *re-* is the onset syllable, *-mem-* is the nucleus, or nuclear syllable, and *-ber* is the coda syllable. There can be only one nuclear syllable in a word but there may be as many as three syllables in the onset or in the coda. Section 8.1 examines various word patterns in this framework and then shows a different kind of analysis, that of Metrical Phonology, which recognizes **metrical feet**, composed of strong and weak syllables.

Some matters in English phonology require us to consider facts outside phonology. Section 8.2 deals with the **morphological structure** of words – the ways in which words may be composed of several meaningful parts: prefixes, bases, suffixes. These considerations are necessary to account for the position of stress in words, taken up in Section 8.3, and the alternation of phonemes in related words, which is the topic of Chapter 12.

In some languages word stress is fixed: stress occurs uniformly on the first, or the last, or the next-to-last (penultimate) syllable of every word. In English there is no such regularity, but the position of the nuclear, or stressed, syllable is often related to specific word-endings, to the part of speech (noun, verb, adjective, etc.), and to the difference between strong and weak syllables. Section 8.3 looks at these 'stress rules.'

8.1 The phonological structure of words: stress patterns

The phonological description of a word includes information about the syllables it has and, if there is more than one syllable, their sequence, and which syllable is stressed. We can use the same terms to describe the structure of a word that we used for describing the structure of a syllable, **onset**, **nucleus**, and **coda**. The stressed syllable is the nucleus, or **nuclear syllable**, of the word; any syllables that precede the nuclear syllable constitute the **onset syllable(s)**; and whatever syllable or syllables follow the nucleus syllable form the **coda syllable(s)** of that word. Nuclear syllable and coda syllable(s) together form the **word rhyme**; that is, *brandy*, *candy*, and *dandy* rhyme with one another, and so do *radium*, *stadium*, and *Palladium*.

The word *den*, considered as a word, has just a nuclear syllable with a zero onset and a zero coda. There are thousands of such one-syllable words in English.

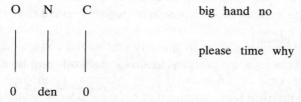

O N C   big hand no

       please time why

0 den 0

The word *canoe* consists of one weak syllable, the onset, and one strong syllable, the nucleus. There is no coda. Numerous words are like this.

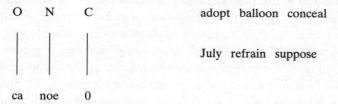

O N C   adopt balloon conceal

       July refrain suppose

ca noe 0

On the other hand, *sofa* has a zero onset and a one-syllable coda.

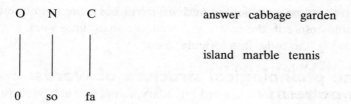

O N C   answer cabbage garden

       island marble tennis

0 so fa

In *abandon* the onset and the coda are each one weak syllable.

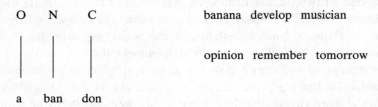

```
O    N    C            banana  develop  musician

|    |    |            opinion  remember  tomorrow


a   ban  don
```

A word may have two weak syllables in the coda, as *elephant* and *humanity* have.

```
O    N    C            algebra  calendar  javelin
|    |   / \           popular  register  vertebra
0    e   le phant
```

```
O    N    C            affectionate  habitual  peripheral
|    |   / \           proprietory  ridiculous  trajectory
hu   ma  ni ty
```

There may be three weak syllables in the coda, as in *adequacy* and *legitimacy*, and *difficulty* (British pronunciation).

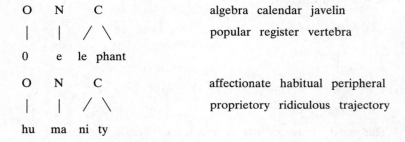

```
O    N      C          gentlemanly  hesitancy  reputable
|    |    /  |  \
0    a   de qua cy

le  gi  ti ma cy       abominable  ineligible  passionately
```

To generalize from these eight patterns, an English word that has one strong syllable, the nucleus, never has more than one weak syllable before it, the onset, and not more than three weak syllables following, the coda. In a formula, then:

(w) N (w) (w) (w)

where '#' stands for the word boundary, initial or final, 'N' is for the nuclear, or stressed, syllable, and 'w' means weak syllable.

Some English words have, in addition to the nuclear syllable, a strong syllable in the onset and/or a strong syllable in the coda.

Notice these words. The onset of each has one strong syllable and zero, one, or two weak syllables:

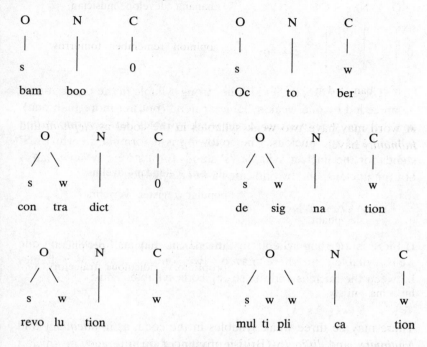

There are words with two strong syllables in the onset, like _prèstidìgitátion_, but of course this is only possible in long words.

Notice these words, each with a strong syllable in the coda and different numbers of weak syllables or none at all:

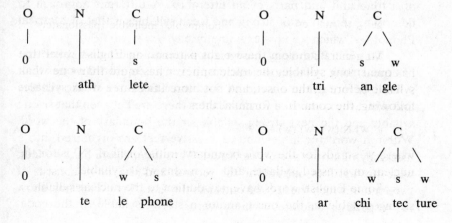

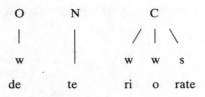

```
    O        N         C
    |        |        / | \
    w        |      w   w   s
   de       te     ri  o  rate
```

To generalize, if there is one strong syllable in the onset, it may be preceded by one weak syllable or none (but not more than one), and there may be two, one, or no weak syllables between that strong syllable and the nucleus. The following is a formula, in which 'N' stands for the nuclear syllable, 's' stands for a strong syllable that is not the nucleus, and 'w' indicates a weak syllable:

$$\# \text{ (w) s (w) (w) N} \dots$$

If there is a strong syllable in the coda, it may be followed by one weak syllable, and there may be two, one, or no weak syllables between the nucleus and the strong coda syllable. Thus:

$$\dots \text{S (w) (w) s (w) } \#$$

The pattern of a word affects the rhythm of the utterance in which it occurs.

This analysis of word stress patterns has used the same terms, onset, nucleus, and coda, to designate parts of a syllable and parts of a word. In succeeding chapters the same terms are used to name parts of a tone unit and parts of an utterance. A different approach to describing sequences of strong and weak syllables is that of Metrical Phonology, which we now examine briefly.

Metrical Phonology recognizes a phonological unit called the (metrical) **foot**. As a phonological unit, it may be a word or less than a word or more than a word. A foot consists of one strong syllable and whatever number of weak syllables there are between that strong syllable and the next strong syllable or the boundary of the word. Within a word (or larger unit) successive feet are organized into a hierarchy of strong versus weak feet. Thus *árchitècture* has two feet, with the first foot outranking the second, and *rèvolútion* consists of two feet, in which the second outranks the first. 'Tree diagrams' show the respective structures of these words.

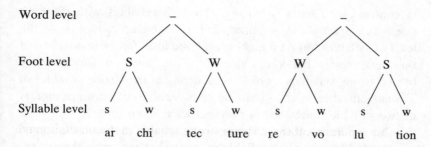

Word level

Foot level

Syllable level

ar chi tec ture re vo lu tion

The stressed syllable of a word, in this scheme, is the strong syllable of a strong foot – or, of course, the strong syllable of the only foot.

A foot may consist of one strong syllable alone or of a strong syllable with a number of weak syllables. The adjective *separate* and the noun *animal* are each a single foot and the verbs *separate* and *animate* are each two feet.

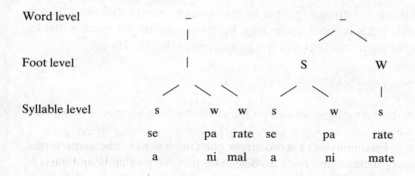

Word level

Foot level

Syllable level

se pa rate se pa rate
a ni mal a ni mate

It is assumed that a foot begins with a strong syllable unless there is a weak syllable at the beginning of a word or phrase. Consider the word *deteriorate*: *de-te-ri-o-rate*. The second syllable and the last syllable are strong and so must belong to separate feet. The initial syllable *de-* must belong to the first foot, but to which foot do the internal weak syllables belong? They, too, belong to the first foot. Presumably, a strong syllable requires a new burst of energy, physiologically, so that, if the notion of 'foot' can be justified as a unit of speech, its physical manifestation is initiation with a strong syllable when that is possible.

The fundamental assumption of Metrical Phonology is that 'strong' and 'weak' can only be relative terms: what is 'strong' is stronger than what is 'weak,' and the term 'weak' is only meaningful in contrast with what is 'strong.' Then, if syllables with different degrees of 'strong' can be noted, their relationship cannot be on the level of syllables but on a higher level, the foot. One consequence of this viewpoint is that words like *athlete* and *bamboo*, which consist of two strong syllables – syllables as strong as the strong syllables of *animate* and *deteriorate* – must be considered to consist, not merely of two syllables each, but of two feet each, even though their relationship to each other is strong–weak in the case of *athlete* and weak–strong for *bamboo*.

PRACTICE 8.1

Here are ten of the word stress patterns presented above. Below are thirty words in alphabetical order, three for each of the ten patterns. Pick out the right words for each pattern.

1 canóe   6 bàmbóo
2 sófa   7 còntradíct
3 abándon   8 télephòne
4 élephant   9 rèvolútion
5 humánity   10 árchitècture

afternoon agriculture appetite apology assemble breakfast campaign cartoon celebrate citizen comedian communism convalesce dandelion democratic divide election entertain exhibition forget furniture legal longitude magnet register remember solicitous tonight upstairs vaccination

8.2 The morphological structure of words

The next section (8.3) deals with rules – general observations – that tell which syllable of a word is the stressed syllable. The rules include information about strong and weak syllables (a phonological matter), part of speech (a syntactic matter), and recognition of different kinds of suffixes (a morphological matter). In this section we investigate something about morphological structure.

A word may consist of just one meaningful part like these:

arm chair happy guitar lemon

or of more than one meaningful part like these:

armchair unhappy guitarist lemonade

The technical term for a minimal meaningful part is **morpheme**. *Arm*, *chair*, *happy*, and *guitar* are all morphemes; none of them can be divided into something smaller that contains a part of the same meaning. They are free morphemes because they occur by themselves, as whole words. The elements *un-*, *-ist*, and *-ade* in *unhappy*, *guitarist*, and *lemonade*, respectively, are also morphemes; they are bound morphemes which are always attached to something else, as in these examples.

With this distinction between free and bound morphemes we recognize four kinds of words. Some consist of a single free morpheme like *arm*, *chair*, *happy*, and *guitar*. We call words that contain just one morpheme **simple words**. Any word that consists of more than one morpheme is a composite word, and we recognize three kinds of composite words:

Type 1. The composite word consists entirely of independent words, free morphemes:

armchair square dance bedroom ice-cold

Words of this type are called **compounds**. Some compounds are written with a hyphen between the parts (e.g. *ice-cold*), some with a space between (e.g. *car key*), and some with neither hyphen nor space (e.g. *scarecrow*). These writing conventions are not entirely logical and have nothing to do with the stress.

Type 2. The composite word consists of one or more independent words, free morphemes, and one or more meaningful parts that are bound morphemes, not independent words:

disarm happiness violinist bus-driver

131

The independent word is called the **base** and a bound morpheme is an **affix**. A type 2 composite consists of at least one base and one affix. An affix that occurs before the base is a **prefix**. An affix that occurs after the base is a **suffix**. These affixes derive new words from simple words. For example, the nouns *baker*, *painter*, *teacher*, and *writer* contain the verbs *bake*, *paint*, *teach*, and *write*, respectively, plus a common suffix *-er* (spelled *-ar* in *beggar* and *liar*, *-or* in *actor*, *governor*, *inspector*, and others). The verbs *uncover*, *unfasten*, *unload*, *unpack*, *untie* contain a prefix *un-* attached to simpler verbs.

Type 3. The composite word consists entirely of bound parts:

    ambigu/ous centi/pede bio/log/y   hexa/gon/al

We can see that these parts are meaningful because we find them occurring in other combinations such as *ambigu/ity*, *gener/ous*, *centi/grade*, *veloci/pede*, *geo/log/ic*, *bio/graph/y*, *hexa/meter*, *octa/gon*.

Type 2 and type 3 words are called **complex**. They represent two different kinds of English words, or what we may call two different strata in the English lexicon. A type 2 word has a neutral suffix or prefix added to an independent word, as in the case of *guitar-ist* and *un-happy*. The stress of *guitarist* is on the same syllable as the stress of *guitar*, and *unhappy* is stressed on the same syllable as *happy*. The pronunciation of *guitar* and *happy* does not change when an affix is added. These affixes are **neutral affixes**.

    A type 3 complex word, on the other hand, has a recognizable prefix or suffix, or both, added to a base that is not an independent word. Often there are several words that have the same base but different suffixes, like the following:

    compete compet-itive compet-ent
    emphas-is emphas-ize emphat-ic
    fratern-al fratern-ity fratern-ize

Addition of a suffix or replacement of one suffix by another causes changes in stress or in the vowel or consonant phonemes of the base, as these examples show. (Quite often it is difficult to define precisely the meaning of a suffix like the *-is* of *emphasis* or the *-on* of *skeleton* but these suffixes are morphemes because they contrast with other suffixes, as in *emphas-ize* or *skelet-al*.) To appreciate the difference between types 2 and 3 compare:

Type 2   re-cover   'to cover again'
Type 3   recover   'to get over an illness; to regain'

Exhibits 8.1 and 8.2 illustrate neutral and non-neutral suffixes, respectively.

EXHIBIT 8.1   Some type 2 suffixes

-al	arrival, burial, denial, dismissal, proposal
-er	announcer, employer, laborer, New Yorker
-ed	bearded, interested, prejudiced, absent-minded
-en	golden, wooden, woolen (adjectives)
-en	cheapen, lengthen, sharpen, strengthen, threaten (verbs)
-ful	cheerful, graceful, joyful, resentful, tactful
-hood	childhood, falsehood, likelihood, motherhood
-ing	absorbing, (un)compromising, interesting, intoxicating
-ish	devilish, feverish, selfish, ticklish
-less	careless, humorless, penniless, relentless
-ly	brotherly, cowardly, friendly, neighborly, slovenly
-ness	consciousness, exactness, heartiness, preparedness
-ship	censorship, hardship, partnership, scholarship
-y	feathery, hungry, silky, (un)wieldy

EXHIBIT 8.2   Some type 3 suffixes

-al	eternal, fatal, general, oriental, radical, universal
-ance, -ence	competence, extravagance, interference, reverence
-ant, -ent	dormant, evident, permanent, prudent, silent, vigilant
-ar	lunar, perpendicular, polar, similar, stellar, triangular
-ate, -ite, -ute	designate, hibernate, ignite, unite, dilute
-esce	acquiesce, coalesce, convalesce, effervesce, rejuvenesce
-fy	amplify, diversify, exemplify, identify, liquefy, personify
-ic	automatic, barbaric, dynamic, economic, periodic
-ics	acoustics, ballistics, calisthenics, economics, semantics
-id	arid, candid, insipid, intrepid, lucid, timid, vivid
-ion	communion, intention, opinion, solution, simplification

133

-ior	anterior, exterior, inferior, interior, junior, senior, superior
-is	catharsis, crisis, emphasis, hypnosis, metropolis
-ish	abolish, astonish, demolish, diminish, extinguish, relinquish
-ive	active, captive, conservative, decisive, negative, permissive
-oid	adenoid, anthropoid, deltoid, rhomboid, spheroid
-or	ardor, candor, color, favor, fervor, rigor, stupor, tremor
-ose	bellicose, comatose, grandiose, jocose, morose
-ous	callous, desirous, disastrous, magnanimous, preposterous
-tude	altitude, exactitude, fortitude, longitude, vicissitude
-ty	absurdity, complexity, humidity, notoriety, society
-um	album, curriculum, decorum, fulcrum, memorandum, platinum, quorum
-ure	censure, composure, departure, lecture, pressure, sculpture
-us	abacus, alumnus, circus, focus, fungus

Note these homophonous suffixes: type 2 *-al* forming nouns, as in *arrival*; type 3 *-al* in adjectives like *eternal*; type 2 *-ish* in adjectives like *feverish*, type 3 *-ish* in verbs like *abolish*.

Then there are some suffixes that occur in type 2 and type 3 complex words. Examples:

absentee, employee, internee	nominee
auctioneer, mountaineer	volunteer
breakable, lovable, readable	amiable, culpable, portable
neutralize, sterilize, modernize	antagonize, mechanize
violinist, naturalist	pessimist, communist
regionalism, parallelism	recidivism, ostracism
employment, argument, inducement	instrument, document
actor, collector, inventor	aggressor, monitor

EXERCISE 8.2

1 Identify each word below as simple or composite, and if composite as type 1, type 2, or type 3.

aspirin bakery colonial hatred postmark telescope

2 Related words that take type 3 suffixes often differ in the place of stress and in whether other syllables are strong or weak; for example:

origin   original   originality
S w w   w S w w   w s w S w w

Here we have used 'S' to mark the stressed syllable, 's' for a strong but unstressed syllable, and 'w' for any weak syllable. Mark the syllables of the following words in the same way.

annual   annuity   admire   admirable   admiration

demolish   demolition   allergy   allergic   allergenic

memorable   memorial   diplomat   diplomacy   diplomatic

contribute   contribution   reside   resident   residential

economy   economical

8.3 Rules for stress in simple words

Repeating the examples used in Section 7.1, *ánimal*, *tomórrow*, *indepéndent*, and *recommendátion* are stressed, respectively, on the first, second, third, and fourth syllables. It may seem that, in English words generally, the nuclear syllable can be any syllable. However, while the position of the stressed syllable is not regular, still it is predictable to a large extent. In this section we examine rules for stress assignment. These 'rules' are simply observations about which syllable is usually stressed in different kinds of words; as you might expect, there are exceptions to the rules. The place of stress in words depends on four kinds of factors operating together:

the form-class (noun, verb, adjective, etc.) of a word;
the number of syllables in a word;
the distinction between strong syllables and weak syllables;
recognition of certain specific prefixes and, especially, suffixes.

The stress of a word may be on the last syllable, the **ult**; on the next-to-last syllable, the **penult**; on the third syllable from the end, the **antepenult**; and a few words are stressed on the fourth syllable from the end, the **pre-antepenult**. In the discussion that follows we consider words in five large groups:

words stressed on the ult;
words stressed on the penult;
words stressed on the penult or antepenult;
words stressed on the antepenult;
words stressed on the antepenult or pre-antepenult.

Obviously words stressed on the antepenult must have at least three syllables and those stressed on the pre-antepenult must have at least four.

Words stressed on the ult (two kinds)

Ult-1. Certain suffixes are always stressed, as in the following:

Nouns	absent*ee*, engin*eer*, techn*ique*
Noun–adjectives	Japan*ese*
Verbs	conval*esce*

(More examples in Exhibit 8.3.)

Ult-2. Verbs and adjectives of two syllables that have a strong ult are stressed on the ult.

agree obey divide promote reduce
attend convict demand except molest
acute divine morose serene

The ult is strong because it has a free vowel or a checked vowel followed by two consonants. Note that all three conditions are necessary: verbs and adjectives with a weak ult are not stressed on the ult (e.g. *covet*, *timid*); two-syllable nouns with a strong ult are not generally stressed on the ult (e.g. *cyclone*); verbs and adjectives with a strong ult but more than two syllables are not stressed on the ult (e.g. *celebrate*, *grandiose*). There are more examples in Exhibit 8.4.

_____ **EXHIBIT 8.3** More examples of Ult-1

Nouns	million*aire* nomin*ee* auction*eer* kitchen*ette*
	phys*ique*
Verbs	acqui*esce*
Adjectives	pictur*esque* un*ique*

_____ **EXHIBIT 8.4** More examples of Ult-2

absurd correct distinct exempt concede debate relate employ
pronounce reply arrest suggest prevent relent

Words stressed on the penult (three kinds)

Penult-1. Verbs and adjectives which have a weak ult:

abandon discover examine inhabit prohibit humid dynamic
explicit insipid periodic

Penult-2. Two-syllable nouns with a strong ult or weak ult:

canine hygiene membrane statute termite hygiene carbine
calcite module delta garden hindrance sentence

There are exceptions. Some two-syllable nouns are stressed on the
ult, for example: *canoe, hotel, machine, police.*

Penult-3. Nouns of two or more syllables that have the suffixes *-ics*
or *-ion*:

civics economics gymnastics physics semantics addition
examination identification indigestion opinion profession
satisfaction solution vision

There are perhaps several dozen nouns that end in *-ics*; there are over
a thousand with *-ion.*

Words stressed on the penult or antepenult (two kinds)

Penult/Antepenult-1. Nouns of more than two syllables that have a weak ult are stressed on the penult if the penult is strong, on the antepenult if the penult is weak.

appendix	horizon	asterisk
intestine	arena	citizen
synopsis	hypnosis	cinema
veranda	aroma	opera

Note that the ult of a noun is weak if it has a checked vowel, even if there are two consonants following as in *appendix* (/-ks/) and *asterisk*. The penult is strong if it ends in a consonant (first column) or has a free vowel (second column); otherwise it is weak (third column).

Penult/Antepenult-2. Adjectives with the suffixes *-al*, *-ant*, *-ent*, *-ine*, *-ous* are stressed on the penult if the penult is strong but on the antepenult if the penult is weak.

abundant	feminine
accidental	generous
internal	magnificent
reluctant	ridiculous
tremendous	vigilant

Words stressed on the antepenult (one kind)

Antepenult-1. Nouns with the suffix *-ty* always have the stress two syllables forward, on the antepenult.

anxiety humility loyalty novelty possibility society

Words stressed on the antepenult or pre-antepenult (two kinds)

Antepenult/Pre-antepenult-1. Most words of three or more syllables with a strong ult are stressed on the antepenult.

Verbs	multiply, prosecute, galivant, implement, manifest
Adjectives	destitute, erudite, grandiose, moribund
Nouns	asteroid, exercise, ridicule, satellite, cellophane, hurricane, dynamite, molecule

However, if the antepenult vowel is followed immediately by the penult vowel, with no consonant between them, stress is on the pre-antepenult.

bibliophile deteriorate heliotrope stereophone

Antepenult/Pre-antepenult-2. A number of nouns and adjectives with certain endings are stressed on the antepenult or pre-antepenult depending on the number of syllables in the word and whether the penult is strong. Let's look at these sets of data:

Suffixes *-acy*, *-ancy*, *-ency*
    fallacy vacancy urgency
    adequacy hesitancy presidency

If there are three syllables, the antepenult is stressed; if there are more, the pre-antepenult gets the stress.

Suffixes *-ary*, *-ory*
    advisory complimentary compulsory trajectory dormitory
    migratory secretary territory

If the antepenult is strong, it is stressed. If not, the pre-antepenult is stressed.

Noun suffix /-i/ (spelled with Y or E), suffix *-m* (syllabic /m/)
    colony energy harmony
    astronomy biology catastrophe facsimile geography
    apoplexy epilepsy matriarchy
    egotism logarithm protoplasm

The antepenult is stressed if the word has only three syllables (first line) or if the penult is weak (second line). If the penult is strong, the pre-antepenult is stressed. This includes all words of four or more syllables that end with a syllabic /m/.

The preceding paragraphs should make the case that there is a certain degree of regularity in the position of the nuclear syllable of a word, and yet the various conditions that determine stress are complex. It would be good to review the 'rules' by grouping the previous statements in a different way:

The suffix is important in determining the position of stress: Ult-1, Penult-3, Penult/Antepenult-2, Antepenult-1, Antepenult/Pre-antepenult-2.

Stress in verbs and adjectives (without suffixes): Ult-2, Penult-1, Antepenult/Pre-antepenult-1.

Stress in nouns (without suffixes): Penult-2, Penult/Antepenult-1.

PRACTICE 8.3

1 Just as the written words *separate* and *compliment* correspond each to two spoken words, the following are also two spoken words. Each is a noun and a verb, pronounced differently:

insult   object   suspect

Verbs are stressed on the second syllable (*to insúlt, to objéct, to suspéct*); nouns are stressed on the first syllable (*an ínsult, an óbject, a súspect*). That seems simple enough but there are numerous exceptions to this generalization. The following, for example, are pronounced alike, with stress on the second syllable, whether noun or verb:

approach   express   reply

Each of the following written words is both noun and verb. Which have different stresses for noun and verb, like *insult*, and which have the same stress, like *approach*?

| command | extract | record |
| contrast | import | subject |

control   overthrow   supply
decay   progress   surprise
exchange   project   survey

2 The list below contains five words that are irregular – not
   stressed on the syllable that should be stressed according to
   our rules. Test your knowledge by finding which words are
   outside the scope of the rules.

Verbs   demolish, exhaust, omit, pollute, prosecute,
             repel
Nouns   adversary, chloride, enamel, enigma,
             metropolis, skeleton
Adjectives   complacent, introductory, permanent,
             preposterous, relative, voluntary

LOOKING BACK

To say that a polysyllabic word is stressed means that one of its
syllables is more prominent than the other(s) and, if the word is in
accented position, that syllable will have the change of pitch; in other
words, stress is the potential for accent. In spite of some dialect
differences, the position of stress in a polysyllabic word is fixed, but
it is not fixed in a numerical sense (always the first or last or next to
last, etc.). In an English word the stressed, or nuclear, syllable may be
preceded by an onset of not more than one weak syllable and
followed by a coda of not more than three weak syllables. The coda
does not have more than one strong syllable, and common words do
not have more than one strong syllable in the onset. There are never
more than two weak syllables between two strong syllables in a word.
Strong endings are defined this way:

Verbs, adjectives   *Nouns*
free vowel   free vowel
two or more final consonants

and have these effects:

Two-syllable V, A	Two-syllable N	More than two syllables
stress ult	stress penult	stress antepenult

The category of 'weak' endings includes those that consist of a single syllable with a checked vowel, final /i, o, u/.

Suggested readings

Fudge (1984: Chapters 3 and 4) has a valuable discussion of word stress, somewhat different from what is presented here. Kreidler (1989: Chapter 11) is similar to the treatment here, with more practice exercises.

Notes

1   Attempts to account for the position of stress in English words can be found at least as far back as Walker (1791). A more modern brief attempt is Arnold (1957) and a much more extensive one is Kingdon (1958a). Chomsky and Halle (1968) presented a set of rules that apply to 'underlying forms' and account for word stress. Their work generated a large number of attempts to refine and improve their statements, including Halle (1973), Dickerson (1975), Fudge (1984), Poldauf (1984), Halle and Vergnaud (1987), and Burzio (1994). All of these have influenced the presentation in this book, but we have tried to favor an account that would be fairly easy to comprehend and to apply rather than one noted for economy or elegance.

2   The origins of Metrical Phonology are in Liberman and Prince (1977). The standard textbook on the topic is Hogg and McCully (1987). Hayes (1995) investigates the relation between rhythm and word stress in a wide range of languages.

Chapter 9

Stress in compound
words and phrases

- **9.1 Noun phrases and noun compounds** 144
- **9.2 Adjective and adverb constructions** 149
- **9.3 Compounds in phrases and larger
  compounds** 152
- **9.4 Verb phrases and verb compounds** 154

LOOKING AHEAD

The last chapter dealt with stress in 'simple' words. Most of those words consisted of a single morpheme, like *answer*, *banana*, or *calendar*; some, like *auctioneer*, *loyalty*, *photographic*, consisted of a base and a suffix, a morpheme that is not a free word. Most of this chapter is about constructions of free words. One kind of construction is syntactic, a phrase; the other is morphological, a compound. Our interest is phonological – how these constructions are stressed and how the stress can change. Section 9.1 looks at noun phrases and noun compounds; in theory these are quite different but some specific items are problematic. Section 9.2 deals with adjective phrases and compounds and adverb phrases and compounds. In Section 9.3 we examine what happens when a compound becomes part of a phrase and when a compound becomes part of a larger compound.

Section 9.4 is about verb compounds, obvious types like *outperform* and *overthrow*, and also constructions that other authors have called phrasal verbs (*stand up*, *turn* the light *out*) and prepositional verbs (*listen to* me).

9.1 Noun phrases and noun compounds

Nouns, verbs, and adjectives are not clearly differentiated in English so that what is apparently one word can belong to two or more of these classes – *comb*, *paint*, *hammer*, and numerous other words are both nouns and verbs; *clean*, *complete*, *warm*, and others function as verb or adjective; *early*, *fast*, and *hard* are adjectives and adverbs. On the other hand, noun phrases, verb phrases, and adjective phrases are constructed in quite different ways, and that is how we know whether a homophonous item is being used as noun, verb, or adjective; compare, for example, *a small black comb with two teeth missing* and *must have been combing her hair*.

Compare these expressions:

déad bírd	déadline	dead énd
bláck cár	bláckberry	black éye

The expressions in the first column are noun phrases; a phrase consists of two or more words; in a phrase such lexical words as *dead*, *bird*, and *black* are stressed and any one of them can be accented. The other expressions are noun compounds. A noun compound is stressed on either the first or the last of its component words. *Déadline* and *bláckberry* have **fore-stress** (they consist of nucleus and coda), *dead énd* and *black éye* have **end-stress** (made up of onset and nucleus). The unstressed word in a compound is strong, or has a strong syllable; however, we leave it unmarked except where there is reason to call attention to stronger versus weaker syllables (see Section 9.3).

In theory phrases and compounds are quite different but in reality some phrases are similar to compounds. Phrases like *this table*, *this machine* are stressed on *this* as well as the following noun, but such frequently used expressions as *this morning*, *this afternoon* are likely to have weak *this*. A phrase can be a long construction with kinds of elements in a very specific order. A noun phrase, or nominal construction, for example, has a noun as head, preceded by a specifier and perhaps one or more modifiers and possibly followed by one or more complements:

specifier	*modifier*	*modifier*	**head**	*complement*	*complement*
some			books		
a	dirty	black	comb	with teeth	
				missing	
the			plate	that is	that you
				broken	mentioned

A short phrase is likely to be part of a tone unit, while a long phrase might be more than one tone unit. The different parts of a phrase can ordinarily be commuted rather freely – that is, starting with *a big plate*, for instance, we can replace *a* with *the*, *this*, *that*, *one*, *each*, and other specifiers; *big* with *clean*, *dirty*, *new*, *expensive*, and numerous other modifiers; *plate* with *bowl*, *table*, *paper*, *car*, and many more nouns. The parts of a phrase can be expanded: *this very clean bowl*, *an even bigger table*, and so on. Commutation and expansion are what make language creative. We can produce and understand an almost infinite number of sentences with a comparatively limited vocabulary. Note also that in a phrase the accent is easily placed on any word: ***this** plate*, *the **big** table*, *an expensive **car***.

A compound, on the other hand, consists of only two elements or of two elements connected with a preposition (*power of attorney, attorney at law*) or a conjunction (*wear and tear, block and tackle*). Apparent exceptions – compounds that seem to consist of three words – are made up of two elements, of which one is itself a compound: *football game, eight-hour day*. The elements of a compound cannot be expanded – you can't say **a very blackberry*, for example – nor can they be commuted extensively. A set of terms like *strawberry, blackberry, raspberry, gooseberry, boysenberry, huckleberry* may seem fairly large, and no doubt botanists or nurserymen will some day create new hybrids and add to the list of berries, but it will always be a limited list. Among adjective compounds a set like *hard-hearted, soft-hearted, warm-hearted, cold-hearted* is similarly finite.

If there is sometimes a problem in deciding whether a given expression is a phrase or a compound, there is a similar problem in distinguishing between compound word and simple word. *Breakfast, cupboard, gentleman*, for instance, are written as if the two parts were still phonologically obvious but they have the pronunciation of simple words. Several place names – for example, *Greenland, Newport, Falmouth* – began as compounds but cannot now be considered as anything but simple words.

Some compounds are written with a hyphen between the parts (e.g. *ice-cold*), some with a space between (e.g. *car key*), and some with neither hyphen nor space (e.g. *scarecrow*). These writing conventions are not entirely logical and have nothing to do with the stress.

An **endocentric compound** is a combination of two simple words that has the syntactic function of one of those words, the head of the construction.

Simple noun	I'm looking for my *keys*.
Compound noun	I'm looking for my *car keys*.
Simple adjective	The water is *cold*.
Compound adjective	The water is *ice-cold*.

In these examples one word provides the general meaning and the other word makes the meaning more specific, and it is easy to see which word is which. A car key is a kind of key, being ice-cold is a specific way of being cold. One member of the compound is generic, and the other is specific. **Exocentric compounds** have the syntactic functions of nouns, verbs, or adjectives but cannot be said to consist of a generic term and a specific term. A scarecrow is neither a crow nor a scare, but *scarecrow* is a noun. *Fireproof* is a compound adjective though neither component is an adjective.

When a compound or a phrase consists of two nouns, the first is in the singular even though it may have plural force in the meaning: a *toothbrush* is a brush for teeth, a *dishwasher* washes dishes, an *eight-hour workday* is a workday of eight hours, etc. Exceptions are nouns that have no singular (*a clothes closet*) or a singular form that has a rather different meaning (*a savings deposit*).

Noun compounds are made up of various parts of speech. Some consist of a particle (*after, back, in, out, up, down, on, off, over, under, through*) plus a noun:

> background downfall intake offshoot overpass outlook upshot underwear   (all fore-stressed; exception: *afternóon*)

Some contain a verb plus a particle, fore-stressed:

> comeback drive-in handout take-off turnover stand-in

A common type has a second element derived from a verb with a suffix *-er* or *-or*; the whole compound names an agent or instrument that drives a bus, washes dishes, etc.

> bus-driver dishwasher history teacher screwdriver tax-collector

Note the stress difference in these two types:

> chéwing gum drínking water sháving cream wáiting room wrápping paper   (*The gum is for chewing*, etc.)
> commanding ófficer flying sáucer revolving dóor traveling sálesman weeping wíllow   (*The officer commands*, etc.)

Some miscellaneous contrasts are seen in Exhibit 9.1. A special group of noun compounds, names of places and organizations, is described in Exhibit 9.2.

EXHIBIT 9.1 Some stress differences in noun compounds ━━━━━━━

báby sitter	baby síster
blóod pressure	blood bróthers
bróther-in-law	attorney-at-láw
hálf-truth	half dóllar
discússion group	group discússion
páper boy	paper dóll

EXHIBIT 9.2 Some proper names ━━━━━━━

Place names and names of organizations often consist of a **generic** name, such as *street*, *avenue*, *river*, *lake*, *canal*, *company*, *society*, and a **specific** name like *Montgomery*, *Arctic*, *National*, *Italian*, etc. In a few cases the generic name comes before the specific name, and the specific name is stressed:

Mount Éverest Lake Louíse Cape Chárles the River Thámes

and all names which have *of* between the generic and the specific:

the Strait of Magéllan the Rock of Gibráltar
the Isthmus of Pánama the University of Califórnia

More often the order is specific before generic, and the generic name is stressed:

Oxford Róad Fifth Ávenue Union Squáre Lovers' Láne
Hyde Párk City Háll Lincoln Túnnel Oxford Univérsity
Trinity Cóllege Trinity Chúrch Canterbury Cathédral
the Rhine Ríver the Himalaya Móuntains the Indian Ócean
the English Chánnel the Technical Ínstitute the Metropolitan
Muséum the Fairfax Hotél the Black Fórest the Gobi Désert
the Panama Canál the European Únion

However, with *street*, *building*, and some words that indicate organizations the specific term comes first and is stressed:

Dówning Street the Wóolworth Building the Fórd Foundation
the Gídeon Society the Sínger Company the Hóover Commission

When a compound and a phrase are composed of the same elements in the same order, usually creating ambiguity in writing, they are of the following types:

Adjective + noun

Phrase:	bláck bírd, gréen hóuse, bríef cáse
Compound:	bláckbird, gréenhouse, bríefcase
Phrase = noun/adjective + noun	Frénch téacher
Compound = noun + agent noun	Frénch teacher
Phrase = adjective (verb-*ing*) + noun	cléaning lády
Compound = gerund (verb-*ing*) + noun	cléaning lady
Phrase = adjective + compound	smáll ánimal hospital
Compound = compound + noun	small ánimal hospital

QUESTION 9.1

Which of these noun compounds are fore-stressed and which are end-stressed?

back seat   blood pressure   bottleneck   civil rights   coffee cup
control tower   crocodile tears   double bed   disease germ
family doctor   front door   full moon   grandfather clock
homework   lifetime   light-year   peanut butter   penny arcade
oak tree   polar bear   self-control   soap suds   tear gas   upper hand

9.2 Adjective and adverb constructions

An adjective phrase has an adjective as head, possibly preceded by a qualifier and followed by a complement.

qualifier	**adjective**	complement
	quiet	
very	studious	
rather	anxious	to leave
	afraid	of his shadow

149

An adjective compound consists of two words. Numerous adjective compounds are end-stressed:

> air-cooled   well bred   self-centered   class-conscious   handmade
> home grown   hard boiled   middle-aged   old-fashioned
> broken-hearted   dead drunk

Some are fore-stressed:

> thoroughbred   knock-kneed   homesick   trustworthy   fireproof
> egg-shaped   bare-headed   near-sighted   henpecked

Others appear in Exhibit 9.3.

EXHIBIT 9.3   Adjective compounds ━━━━━━━━━━━━━

The compounds in the left-hand column are among those that are stressed on the second element when used predicatively (as in *This coat is brand-néw*) but have greater stress on the first element when used attributively (as in *This is a brànd-new coat*). The ones in the right-hand column are stressed on the first element in either position.

brand-new	air-conditioned
crystal-clear	airborne
dirt-cheap	bloodthirsty
easy-going	color-blind
hand-picked	footloose
hardworking	frost-bitten
ice-cold	full-scale
jet-propelled	headstrong
knee-deep	heart-broken
old-fashioned	lived-in
run-down	outgoing
well-bred	tongue-tied

Adverbial phrases are similar to adjectival phrases except that they do not have a complement.

qualifier | **adverb**
        happily
quite   recently

Adverb compounds are similar to prepositional phrases. A prepositional phrase has a preposition, optionally preceded by a modifier, followed by a noun phrase.

modifier	**preposition**	noun phrase
	in	the park
right	between	Jason and Janet
just	outside (of)	our house
	because of	a recent snowstorm

So *down the stream*, *up the stairs* are prepositional phrases, *downstream* and *upstairs* are adverb compounds. Other examples, which are end-stressed when pronounced in isolation, are:

downtown indoors outside backstage overhead underfoot

A compound may be part of a phrase, as head (*big blackbird*) or as modifier (*downtown traffic*) and a compound can be part of a compound (see above). The phrase *a tall cabinet* refers to a cabinet that is tall. The phrase *a tall bookcase* refers to a bookcase that is tall, not a case for tall books.

QUESTION 9.2

1 Which of these adjective compounds are stressed on the first element and which on the second?

well-mannered seasick praiseworthy poverty-stricken
good-looking easy-going tax-free self-conscious
undernourished

2 There is a small group of compound pronouns and a few similar adverb compounds. How are they stressed?

anybody anywhere everybody everything everywhere
somebody somehow something somewhere someone

How do these pronouns differ from the above?

myself himself herself yourself yourselves

9.3 Compounds in phrases and larger compounds

Adjective and adverb compounds which are part of the predicate or follow the predicate have stress on the second element but, when they precede a noun, stress is either even on both elements or else the first element gets the stress.

> The book is overdúe.
> an òverdùe bóok
> an òverdue bóok

Consequently, adjective compounds that are used predicatively more than attributively are usually cited as after-stressed, and those that are mostly used attributively are thought of as fore-stressed.

A compound can be part of a larger compound, for example: *fingernail polish, football team, life insurance policy*. Each of these has a fore-stressed compound (*fingernail, football, life insurance*) as the first element of a larger compound which is itself fore-stressed. We can show the layers of construction in *fingernail polish* this way, with O standing for 'onset,' N for 'nucleus,' and C for 'coda':

```
fingernail  polish
N      C
 N              C
```

That is, *finger* outranks *nail* in the compound *fingernail*, and this compound outranks *polish* in the compound *fingernail polish*. The construction of *football team* and *life insurance policy* is the same, ignoring different numbers of weak syllables in the words.

We can even have a compound within a compound within a compound, like *fingernail polish remover*.

```
fingernail  polish  remover
N      C
 N              C
        N               C
```

Taking this construction apart, *fingernail polish remover* consists of stronger *fingernail polish* and weaker *remover*; *fingernail polish* is made up of the stronger *fingernail* and weaker *polish*; *fingernail* is a compound of strong *finger* and weak *nail*. This morphologic construction on three levels might suggest that there are numerous degress of stress in the compound. Actually, the pronunciation can be represented this way:

```
S  w  s     s w     w s w
fingernail  polish  remover
```

Such long compounds are of course less common than short ones. Short compounds may have various constructions:

a fore-stressed compound (*sídewalk*) as the first part of an end-stressed compound: *sidewalk café*;

an end-stressed compound (*missing pérsons*) as the first part of a fore-stressed compound: *missing pérsons bureau*;

an end-stressed compound (*peanut bútter*) as the first part of an end-stressed compound: *peanut butter sándwich*;

an end-stressed compound (*peanut bútter*) as the first part of an end-stressed compound (*peanut butter and jélly*), which is the first part of an end-stressed compound: *peanut butter and jelly sándwich*.

```
sidewalk café              missing persons bureau
 N  C                        O    N
   O     N                    N          C
```

```
peanut butter sandwich
 O    N
    O       N
```

```
       peanut butter and jelly sandwich
        O    N
          O       N
            O          N
```

A compound can be the head of a phrase:

a green necktie   delicious pancakes   typically home-grown

A compound may be composed of two compounds:

five-dollar taxi-ride
Conservative Party planning committee

Here are phrases composed of a modifier and a head, in which the modifier is a compound:

(gréenhòuse) grèenhòuse dóor *or* grèenhouse dóor
(pèanut bútter) pèanut bùtter sándwich *or* pèanut butter sándwich
(pèanut bùtter and jélly) pèanut butter and jèlly sándwich

In other words, when a compound with fore-stress (s w) or with end-stress (w s) occurs before the head of a phrase (S), stress in the compound is leveled out

s w S → s w S   w s S → s w S

More examples:

càmel's hair cóat   còuntry club dánce   wèekend tríp
càrdboard cóver   èlderberry wíne

The same is true when the head of the construction is itself a compound:

five-dollar táxi-ride   Mìssing Persons Búreau chief

QUESTION 9.3

What is the inner structure of these constructions?

income tax return
post office clerk
seeing-eye dog
five-year plan
medical technician training program

9.4 Verb phrases and verb compounds

Verb phrases occur in various types. One common type has the verb *be* with various kinds of complements – noun phrase, adjective phrase, or prepositional phrase.

auxiliaries	**be**	complement
	is	a banker
has	been	very happy
must	be	under the sideboard

Another kind of verb phrase has a verb with no complement, one complement, or two complements, depending on what the verb is.

auxiliaries	**verb**	complement	complement
	snores		
is	playing	checkers	
must be	writing	a letter	to the bank
should have	put	the car	in the garage

We have seen that noun compounds which have a particle (*after*, *down*, *in*, *off*, *on*, *out*, *over*, *under*, *up*) as first element are stressed on that element; verb compounds with these particles as first element have end-stress.

Nouns	afterthought, downfall, infield, onset, outgrowth, overcoat, underbrush, upkeep
Verbs	infringe, outgrow, overcome, undergo, uphold

There are several noun–verb pairs, written alike, which differ in speech because the nouns are stressed on the first syllable, the verbs on the second:

offset overflow overlap overthrow overlook upset upturn

Some other contrasts between noun and verb:

fóllow-up	follow úp
grównup	grow úp
ónlooker	look ón

There are not many verb compounds that do not have a particle. Some of them are simply nouns converted to verbs (*to air-condition*, *to dead-end*, *to horsewhip*) or derived from nouns by back-formation (*to babysit* from *babysitter*, *to window-shop* from *window-shopping*).

English has quite a lot of composite verbs made up of a verb followed by a particle or a preposition or both a particle and a preposition, for example:

1   verb + particle, intransitive

     sit down   stand up   look out

2   verb + particle, transitive

     (a)   put on (your hat)   turn off (the light)   look up (a word)
     (b)   get on (the bus)   go with (a friend)

3   verb + preposition, transitive

     look at (pictures)   listen to (music)   wait for (a friend)

4   verb + particle + preposition, transitive

     put up with (this nonsense)   do away with (these rules)
     look up to (our heroes)

These are sometimes called phrasal verbs but that term seems to imply that *look óut*, for example, is a phrase whereas *lóok-out* is a noun compound. It seems more sensible to call both *look óut* and *lóok-out* compounds, verb compound and noun compound, respectively. In the same way the participle form *run-dówn* is an adjective compound, a *rún-down* is a noun compound, and *to run dówn* (what a clock may do, for instance) is a verb compound.

Intransitive compounds (group 1) are normally stressed on the particle.

     He stood úp, walked óut, turned aróund, and looked báck.

Transitive compounds of group 2a are separable. The noun phrase that functions as object of the verb may come either after the particle or between verb and particle. Stress is on the head of the noun phrase.

     She took off her cóat | and put on a swéater.
     She took her cóat off | and put a swéater on.

If the object is a pronoun, it must precede the particle, which carries the stress.

> She took it óff.
> She put them ón.

Verbs of group 2b are not separable. If the object is (or contains) a noun, the noun is stressed. If the object is a pronoun, the particle is stressed.

> They got on the bús.   They got ón it.
> I'm going with Sára.   I'm going wíth her.

Verb compounds of group 3 consist of a verb and a preposition. The preposition is not ordinarily stressed (but Chapter 10 describes the less ordinary instances in which such function words are stressed).

> We looked at the píctures.   We lóoked at them.
> We'll wait for Júlia.   We'll wáit for her.

As the examples show, the sequence of preposition + pronoun does not bear stress, so the preceding word, the verb, is stressed.

With group 4 compounds, verb + particle + preposition, the facts are almost the same. A noun as object gets the stress; a sequence of preposition + pronoun is not stressed, so that stress falls on the preceding word, which is the particle.

> I'm not going to put up with these trícks.
> I'm not going to put úp with them.

Next we consider what happens when a transitive compound verb occurs at the end of a tone unit.

> Group 2   What coat did she put ón?
>   Which bus did they get ón?
> Group 3   What records have you lístened to?
>   Is this what he ásked for?
> Group 4   This sort of nonsense we won't put úp with.

The rule is simple: a particle in final position is stressed. A final preposition is not stressed, and stress falls on whatever strong word precedes it.

QUESTION 9.4

The words *at*, *for*, *of*, *to*, and *with* are always prepositions. The word *on* is sometimes a particle and sometimes a preposition. The following sentences have compound verbs in which the second element is *on*. In which instances is *on* a particle? In which is it a preposition?

I insist on a full report by tomorrow.
Professor Smedley refused to comment on that topic.
Switch on that table lamp, will you?

LOOKING BACK

Phrases and compounds are constructions generated by the grammar of the language; we have examined noun phrases, adjective phrases, prepositional phrases, and verb phrases, and noun compounds, adjective compounds, adverb compounds, and verb compounds. Compounds consist of two items, possibly joined by a preposition or conjunction; phrases consist of two or more words filling three principal positions: specifier, head, and complement. In a phrase every lexical item is stressed and any of them can be accented.

A compound word is stressed on the first word (fore-stress) or the last word (end-stress). Noun compounds with fore-stress are more numerous than those with end-stress. Compound verbs which consist of a verb and a particle have greater stress on the particle; those which consist of verb and preposition have greater stress on the verb. Adverb compounds and many adjective compounds are end-stressed when they occur in predicative position – typically the end of a verb phrase. In attributive position, where the compound precedes the head of a noun phrase, stress is leveled out and may shift to the first element of the compound.

Suggested readings

Fudge (1984: Chapter 5) has an extensive treatment of stress in compounds. Adams (1973: Chapters 5–9) treats stress and also analyzes syntactic formation of compounds. Bauer (1983) and Marchand (1969) are thorough descriptions of word formation in English, including compounding, but do not deal much with the matter of stress.

Chapter 10

The role of accent
in discourse

- **10.1 The structure of a tone unit**   162
- **10.2 Tonality**   164
- **10.3 Tonicity**   166

LOOKING AHEAD

An utterance consists of one or more tone units, and each tone unit has an intonation and one accented syllable, the nucleus of the tone unit. Two utterances that contain the same words in the same sequence may differ in **prosody**: they may be spoken with different melodies, or intonations; they may be divided into different numbers of tone units, which means different numbers of accents; or, within any tone unit, the accent may be in different places. Intonation is taken up in Chapter 11; the other matters are the subject of Section 10.1. (We continue to use the downward arrow (↓) and upward arrow (↑) to represent falling and rising intonations, respectively. Chapter 11 introduces other symbols for more complex intonations.)

The accented word in a tone unit carries the most important information, new information, and generally this word is at the end of the tone unit. When an earlier word is accented, the accent creates a special focus. One reason for this focus is to highlight a contrast with something previously said. Within a word the stress and accent may shift to a prefix that is in contrast with another prefix or with no prefix. (See Section 10.2.)

However, a word may be accented, not so much because it is important, but because other parts are de-accented: they present old information, repeating what has been said earlier in the discourse. Languages have special forms called **anaphoric words** to express what has already been mentioned. (See Section 10.3.)

10.1 The structure of a tone unit

In speech meanings are communicated not merely by what is said but also by the way it is said. We humans have invented ways of preserving our sayings through writing, but the writing systems that we have do not reflect all that is present in speech. Writing indicates consonant and vowel phonemes with some degree of accuracy, but no language has a writing system that adequately represents the rhythms and melodies of our utterances. Punctuation marks, italics, and underlining are crude ways of trying to represent these prosodic elements that provide nuances of meaning in what we say.

If prosodic elements have a role in communication, then they must be shared by members of the language community. There are personal differences in the ways that people speak, and there are dialect differences, but there are also ways of talking which are common to all speakers of the language. By using differences in the 'tone of voice' we convey different messages which, by and large, are recognized and reacted to by all speakers of the language. These ways of using the voice form the prosody, or prosodic system, of English.

An utterance can be quite short, consisting of a single tone unit, even just one word, but most utterances consist of several tone units. When we speak, unless we are reciting from a prepared script, we all make slips of the tongue, hesitate, repeat, and have to make corrections but in general we manage to deliver the message we intend. Similarly, we understand what others have to say in spite of their linguistic lapses. As pointed out in Chapter 3, when we listen to someone talking (in a language we know), we don't simply hear one sound after another nor even one word after another; we unconsciously organize the message into units of information, tone units, which reflect the grammatical structure of the utterance. Of course, there is no simple correlation between a unit of information and a tone unit; if there were, everyone would deliver the same information in exactly the same way at all times. Instead of that, because of the variety of personalities and the variety of circumstances in which we use language, we differ in the tempo and manner of our speaking and in what we want to emphasize.

Prosody is concerned with three matters:

1   The tune or **intonation** of utterances. Repeating a pair of simple examples from Chapter 7, there is a difference between *Ann ↓léft* and *Ann ↑léft* – that is, a difference in intonation only. (In the rest of this chapter we will use only one acute diacritic (´) in each tone unit, indicating only the accented syllable.)

2   **Tonality**, or how speakers divide utterances into tone units.

Each tone unit has one accented syllable and therefore one accented word which gets special attention or focus. Thus, the more numerous the divisions made in an utterance – the more tone units there are – the more points of emphasis there are. Compare "I'd never say ↓thát" with one focus and "Í | would néver | say ↓thát" with three. (The vertical mark, |, is used to separate tone units.) These utterances differ only in tonality. If the utterance is broken into two or more sense groups, each group has its own accent. The last accent is ordinarily the most prominent of all because the pitch changes on that syllable.

3   **Tonicity**, the position of the accented word within a tone unit. Compare these utterances: "Roger said he would hélp us" and "Roger sáid he would help us." These differ only in tonicity.

10.2 Tonality

There is no precise relation between a sentence or a clause, which are grammatical units, and an utterance or a tone unit, which are phonological units. A tone unit may include a whole clause, but a clause can be broken into two or more tone units. Obviously, the longer an utterance and the slower the speech, the more tone units the utterance will have. There are no absolute 'rules' about separating utterances into tone units – tonality – but we can make some observations about what is often done.

(a)   Mr Moore's fírst name | is Básil, | ísn't it?
(b)   Yés, | and he's forty-five years óld.
(c)   He's márried | and has three chíldren.
(d)   His wife is named Bétty, | I thínk.
(e)   Shé's forty-five, | tóo.

A speaker can separate subject and predicate as in (a) but doesn't need to if the subject is short, as it is in this case. Two clauses can be separated, as in (c), but, since they are short, the utterance could be a single tone unit. The following are generally separate tone units:

tag questions, like *isn't it?* (a), *don't they?*, *shouldn't we?*;
tag comments like *I think* (d), *it seems*, *perhaps*;
introductory remarks such as *Yes* (b), *No*, *Of course*, *As a matter of fact*;

the words *too* (e) and *either*;
a vocative such as *Mary*, *Mr Moore*, *sir*, *darling*, whether at the
    beginning of the utterance or at the end.

Tonality can make a difference of meaning. The following pairs
of utterances are alike except for the number of tone units they have;
tonality makes distinctions.

I learned about the accident from my cóusin, I who lives in Chátham.
I learned about the accident from my cousin who lives in Chátham.

(The distinction between a non-restrictive clause and a restrictive
one.)

The postman left four létters I and a package for Dávid.
The postman left four letters and a package for Dávid.

(These would not be distinguished in writing, creating ambiguity; how
many items has David received from the postman?)

They didn't léave I because they were ángry.
They didn't leave because they were ángry.

(Again, an ambiguity in writing unless a comma or dash is inserted to
make the first utterance tell why 'they' left; does *didn't* go with *leave*
or with all the rest of the utterance?)

She wáshed I and combed her háir.
She washed and combed her háir.

(Are there two verb phrases or one verb phrase with a compound
verb?)

My bróther I Péter I and Dénnis I had a big árgument.
My brother Péter I and Dénnis I had a big árgument.

(In written form the first sentence would have commas before and
after *Peter*, thus clarifying the number of people involved in the
argument.)
    No doubt these examples seem contrived, and indeed they are,
because we don't encounter such contrasting pairs in our day-to-day

experience with language. Tonality can remove ambiguity, but this is not to say that we consistently use tonality to remove ambiguity. Ambiguity may be a problem in writing – in laws and contracts, for example – and it may be a source of humor for the comedian, but in ordinary conversation we are often not even aware of ambiguity. We correctly interpret what a speaker means from the context in which an utterance occurs. Nevertheless, language is a system of contrasts. To understand how a language works we need to see what minimal contrasts there are, even though we don't often encounter such contrasts in ordinary use of language.

QUESTION 10.1

Could each of the following utterances be a single tone unit? If not, what would be a likely way to divide each one that needs dividing?

What this city needs is better public transportation.
It needs much more than that, I'd say.
First of all, the police are underpaid.
The firemen need more modern equipment.
We don't have enough ambulances, either.

10.3 Tonicity

An utterance is ordinarily part of a larger discourse, and to understand the utterance we have to relate what is being said to what was said previously. In any discourse something new is always being said and, after the first utterance, there is generally some reference to what has been said previously. Thus an utterance is likely to contain new information and old, or given, information.

Every tone unit has one accented word; that word is the most informative word, and usually that word – the nucleus of the tone unit – comes at or near the end of the tone unit. "There's just been a terrible áccident" is much more likely than "A terrible áccident has just happened." Notice that the noun phrase *a terrible accident* is indefinite. That is the way we usually introduce a new topic.

There are exceptions. Notice that the following utterances have the accented word at the beginning.

The télephone is ringing.
The bús is coming.
Tómmy's here!

Each of these utterances could be spoken in isolation – could be a whole discourse by itself. Each has a definite noun phrase as subject, followed by a very short predicate. A definite noun phrase indicates that the speaker assumes the addressee can identify the referent of the noun phrase, because the situation makes the information 'given'; there is no need, in these cases, to tell what telephone or bus or to identify the person named Tommy. Quite often we produce an isolated utterance like these, calling attention to some person or thing (the subject) and making a brief comment about that person or thing (the predicate). In such instances the subject is typically accented.

In a sustained discourse, however, at least after the first few utterances, new information is typically introduced late in an utterance – including reference to people and things – so that a name will be accented when first spoken: "I saw Bob Dávison last night"; but that entity, once introduced, will be referred to by such function words as *he, she, it, they, that one, these.* New information is rarely introduced in subject position.

Let's illustrate how one utterance can have different tonicity – have a different nuclear word in different contexts. Suppose you were to say,

(a)   I've just seen a ghóst.

If someone replied "There's no such thing as a ghost," a likely rejoinder might be:

(b)   Oh yés? | Well, I've séen a ghost.

To the statement "Oh, you haven't seen a ghost," a possible reply would be

(c)   Oh yés. | I háve seen a ghost.

On the other hand, in reply to the statement "Nobody has seen a ghost," you might say:

(d)   Í've seen a ghost.

To say that the accent is in a different place in these four tone units is the same as saying that the nucleus of the tone unit is in a different place. The structure of these four tone units can be shown this way:

Tone unit structure

	Onset	Nucleus	Coda
(a)	I've just seen a	ghóst.	
(b)	I've	séen	a ghost.
(c)	I	háve	seen a ghost.
(d)		Í've	seen a ghost.

There has to be an accent somewhere in a tone unit. Let's say that utterance (a) represents a kind of norm: the whole utterance is informative in itself; nothing in it refers to something previously said, and accent is on the last word in the tone unit. We call this the neutral, or unmarked, occurrence of accent. When accent occurs earlier in the tone unit, it indicates some special function; it is a marked occurrence. Utterances (b), (c), and (d) show such special functions.

In utterance (b) the speaker, responding to "There's no such thing as a ghost," accents *seen* ("I've séen a ghost") or more precisely de-accents what follows, *a ghost*, because that phrase has just been mentioned; it is old information, therefore not accented.

Utterance (c) de-accents *seen a ghost* because all of this was in the utterance to which the speaker is responding. But there is more here: by accenting *have* the speaker creates a contrast with the word *haven't* in the previous utterance, emphasizing the truth of what is said. Paraphrasing loosely, "I háve seen a ghost" means "It is not true that I haven't seen a ghost; it is true that I have (done so)."

Utterance (d) is an obvious instance of contrast. Responding to "Nobody has seen a ghost," we have "Í've seen a ghost." Here *have seen a ghost* is de-accented because it repeats old information and *I* is highlighted to emphasize the contrast with *nobody*.

Since language is a system, we need to consider the ways words are related to one another. One relationship is **syntagmatic**, the associations of words in the same tone unit or utterance. What a word means depends on what its associates are.

> The jeweler carefully placed the stone in the ring.
> The mason carefully placed the stone in the wall.

Stone means rather different things in these two utterances.

Another relationship is **paradigmatic**, the association between one word and other words that might contrast with it in the same utterance. What an item means is in part dependent on what it is not.

> Shirley wrote a long letter to her ____ .

The blank can be filled with *mother, cousin, friend, teacher, employer, husband,* and a good number of other nouns, which together form a paradigmatic set.

Notice, then, that marked occurrence of accent has two inter-related functions. When the accent does not occur at the end of a tone unit, it may emphasize one word in contrast to some other word in a previous utterance (or to some other word that might be said), as *I* in utterance (d) above contrasts with *nobody*. Or the accent may fall on one word within the tone unit because some other part of the tone unit, especially what follows, represents old information. Thus, in utterance (b) accent is on *seen* because what follows is not new. And in utterance (c) accent performs both functions together: the accented *have* contrasts with the previous *haven't* and at the same time what follows, *seen a ghost*, is de-accented.

In paradigmatic focus the speaker is contrasting, explicitly or implicitly, one word or term with other possible words or terms of the same grammatical and semantic set. The word or term is highlighted with respect to other items of the language that might occupy the same position in the utterance. One kind of paradigmatic focus is a shift of stress forward in certain compound words. Used alone, each of these words is stressed on the ult:

> insíde outdóors upstáirs downtówn
> thirtéen . . . ninetéen

However, when there is contrast, stress advances:

> ínside | or óutside

> úpstairs | and dównstairs
> fífteen, | síxteen, | séventeen, | éighteen

Similarly, stress advances to a prefix when the prefix contrasts with its absence – with zero. For example, *dislíke* and *retéll* are normally stressed as marked, but:

> I don't líke them | but I don't díslike them.
> He told and rétold the story.

In syntagmatic focus, on the other hand, one word or term is highlighted with respect to other items of the same utterance. These non-highlighted items are de-accented because they contribute little or nothing to the information conveyed in the utterance. Most often, de-accented words refer to some previously used linguistic form and thus carry information which is already 'given,' not 'new.' Therefore, a word may be accented, not because it is important or contrastive, but because what follows is old information. Another example will clarify.

> You'll find all the information you need in the líbrary.
> Where ís the library?

The word *is* is certainly not accented here because it is important or in contrast with something else. It is accented because what follows repeats what was previously mentioned.

Paradigmatic and syntagmatic focus often co-occur:

> Are you wearing your brówn suit | or your blúe suit?

Here *blue* contrasts with *brown* and so has paradigmatic focus but it has syntagmatic focus with respect to what follows.

Most often, de-accented words are **anaphoric**, referring to some previously used linguistic form and thus carrying information which is already 'given,' not 'new.'

Let's repeat the utterances about seeing a ghost in a slightly different format.

(a)   I've just seen a ghóst.
      (There's no such thing as a ghost.)
(b)   Oh yés? | Well, I've séen one.

A substitute word like *one* ties an utterance to an earlier part of the discourse; it is a linguistic device that stands for whatever singular noun phrase has last been uttered, in this case a *ghost*.

(Oh, you haven't seen a ghost.)
(c)   Oh yés. | I háve (done).

Instead of "I háve seen a ghost," some speakers of English might say, with the same effect, "I háve done," using the function word *done* in place of *seen a ghost* (or, putting it better, using the function word *do*, with the necessary adjustment, in place of *see a ghost*). Other speakers of English might say, simply, "I háve," in which nothing at all, zero, stands for the information about seeing a ghost.

(Nobody's seen a ghost.)
(d)   Í have (done).

Instead of "Í've seen a ghost," the predicate, which is old information, can be replaced with the shorter utterance "Í have" or "Í have done," a function word or words taking the place of the whole predicate.

The following shows the structure of the four tone units when anaphoric items are used.

Tone unit structure

	Onset	Nucleus	Coda
(a)	I've just seen a	ghóst.	
(b)	I've	séen	one.
(c)	I	háve	(done).
(d)		Í	have (done).

Languages have anaphoric words whose function is to refer to what has previously (and recently) been communicated in a different way. Some of the anaphoric words in English are shown in Exhibit 10.1.

_____

EXHIBIT 10.1 Anaphoric words

_____

1   The pronouns *he*, *she*, *it*, and *they*, which replace definite noun phrases:

with Gregory | or withóut $\begin{cases} \text{Gregory} \\ \text{him} \end{cases}$

2   The pronouns *one* and *some*, which are typically strong and which replace indefinite noun phrases:

We wanted to buy a néwspaper I and we fóund $\begin{cases} \text{a newspaper.} \\ \text{one.} \end{cases}$

We looked for magazínes I and fóund $\begin{cases} \text{magazines.} \\ \text{some.} \end{cases}$

3   The pronoun *one, ones*, which is weak and which replaces a countable noun after certain modifiers:

Are you wearing your blúe suit I or your brówn $\begin{cases} \text{suit?} \\ \text{one?} \end{cases}$

Are you wearing brówn shoes I or bláck $\begin{cases} \text{shoes?} \\ \text{ones?} \end{cases}$

4   Nothing – zero – replacing a non-countable noun:

Do your prefer wárm milk I or cóld $\begin{cases} \text{milk?} \\ \text{0?} \end{cases}$

5   Zero replacing any noun after a possessive word:

Dora's birthday's in Márch I and Dón's $\begin{cases} \text{birthday I is in Júne.} \\ \text{0.} \end{cases}$

6   The adverbs *there* and *then*, which replace place phrases and time phrases, respectively:

I expected to meet our guests at the áirport I
but I didn't fínd $\begin{cases} \text{our guests} \\ \text{them} \end{cases}$ $\begin{cases} \text{at the airport.} \\ \text{there.} \end{cases}$

In addition to function words with an anaphoric purpose we can also recall previous information by using lexical words.

There was a strange statue in the córner.

I walked over to exámine $\begin{cases} \text{the statue.} \\ \text{the sculpture.} \\ \text{the thing.} \\ \text{it.} \end{cases}$

Given information can be recalled by repeating the term (*the statue*), by using a synonym (*the sculpture*), by using a superordinate – a more general, inclusive term (*the thing*), or a grammatical word that has just this function (*it*). The first three are instances of lexical anaphora; the last is an example of grammatical anaphora. In any case, the anaphoric item is de-accented, and the de-accenting is what tells us that the words are being used anaphorically.

When a word that is normally anaphoric is accented, it indicates a contrast or a selection from among two or more possibilities. Compare:

(a)	Do you know Mrs Lándon?	Yés, ǀ I knów her.
(b)	Do you know Mr and Mrs Lándon?	Wéll, ǀ I know hér.
(c)	Have you visited the Árt Museum?	Nó, ǀ I haven't béen there.
(d)	Have you visited the Árt Museum?	I haven't been thére.

In the last response the accent on *there*, especially if spoken with a fall–rise intonation (Section 11.2), carries the implication that the speaker has visited other places in the same category as the Art Museum.

Finally, note the subtle meanings that can be delivered by accenting a form of the verb *be* or an auxiliary verb (*have*, *do*, *can*, *could*, *will*, *would*, *may*, *might*, *shall*, *should*, *must*) as shown in Exhibit 10.2. The accent may emphasize the meaning of the auxiliary verb, or the tense that the verb indicates, or it may focus on polarity, stressing that the utterance is negative or affirmative, as in our previous example, "I háve seen a ghost."

PRACTICE 10.2

Utterances below are in sets of two or more. The utterances in each set have the same verbal content but differ in tonicity – that is, perhaps in what they say and perhaps in how they are related to different contexts. For each set explain how the utterances might differ.

1 (a) Manuel's English is almost pérfect.
  (b) Manuel's English is álmost perfect.
  (c) Manuél's English is almost perfect.

2 (a) Where did you eat lúnch?
  (b) Where díd you eat lunch?
3 (a) Polly plays the flúte, | tóo.
  (b) Pólly plays the flute, | tóo.
4 (a) Did you say fourtéen?
  (b) Did you say fóurteen?
5 (a) Herbert said he would méet us here.
  (b) Herbert sáid he would meet us here.

EXHIBIT 10.2 Accent on auxiliaries and *be*

Is Jack going to finish this jób?
He máy finish, | he cán finish, | he shóuld finish, | but wíll he? | I don't knów.

These accents emphasize the meanings of the auxiliaries.

Is Jack in the óffice now?
I don't knów. | He wás there.

Here the accent on a form of *be* emphasizes the meaning of past tense, contrasting with the present tense of the question.

If Jack had been in the óffice, | he would have finished the wórk.
He wás in the office | and he díd finish the work.

Here the accent affirms that these are the true facts, as contrasted with the hypothetical statement that preceded. This 'accent of insistence' falling on *be* and auxiliary *have* requires the full form of those verbs.

You're wróng.   You áre wrong.
The plane's lánded.   The plane hás landed.

When an utterance has neither *be* nor an auxiliary, the auxiliary *do* is 'imported' to carry the accent that expresses insistence.

I belíeve you.   I dó believe you.

LOOKING BACK

Communication through speech makes use of sequences of words in grammatical constructions and also prosodic elements. An utterance consists of one or more tone units, each with its intonation and accented word. Two utterances with the same sequence of words may still differ in tonality, the number of tone units into which they are divided; in tonicity, the location of the accent in one or more tone units; and in intonation.

Longer utterances are likely to consist of more tone units than shorter utterances, but tonality also depends on the tempo and style of speech and the number of words a speaker chooses to emphasize. Divisions between tone units generally coincide with divisions between phrases or clauses. We have examined pairs of sentences which have the same sequence of words but which differ grammatically – and therefore semantically – because they differ in how many tone units they have or where the division between tone units occurs.

A short, isolated utterance that consists of a definite noun phrase as subject followed by a brief predicate may have the accent on the subject. On the other hand, more extended discourse typically consists of utterances, each of which (after the first) contains some new information and some old, or given, information. Typically, new information comes near the end of an utterance or tone unit and the main word in which it is expressed gets the accent. When accent falls on an earlier word, this is due to one or both of two kinds of focus, paradigmatic and syntagmatic. Paradigmatic focus is deliberate contrast. The speaker chooses to make one term stand out as distinct from some other term of the same grammatical and semantic category. Paradigmatic focus includes the shift of stress to a (normally unstressed) prefix for contrast with another prefix or with zero. Paradigmatic focus also includes polarity emphasis, accent on an auxiliary verb that carries the meaning of 'affirmative' or 'negative.'

Syntagmatic focus is accent that occurs on a word simply because what follows is old information and therefore de-accented. Old information may be presented in the lexical items that have already been used in the discourse or through anaphora. Grammatical anaphora is the use of special function words, the purpose of which is to refer back to what has occurred earlier in the discourse. Lexical anaphora is the use of synonyms or superordinate terms for this purpose.

Non-final accent may have both a paradigmatic and a syntagmatic purpose.

Note

The terms 'tonality' and 'tonicity' originated in Halliday (1967).

Chapter 11

Intonation

- **11.1 Paralanguage**   178
- **11.2 Intonations of the simple tone unit**   180
- **11.3 Low and high onsets**   186
- **11.4 Compound tunes**   187

LOOKING AHEAD

Intonation is part of the language system. When anyone speaks, there are features of the voice that we call paralanguage and which are not truly part of language. Like gestures and other visual phenomena, paralanguage leads us to form some opinion of the speaker and hence of his/her message, but these elements are not systematic. (See Section 11.1.)

The elements of intonation are changes in the frequency of vibration of the vocal cords, centering on the accented syllable. We recognize falling and rising tunes of different lengths and combinations of such rises and falls. In general, falling tunes suggest finality; they are used when the speaker asserts something or, in a question, is confident of an answer. Rising tunes are more oriented toward the addressee and suggest openness (Section 11.2). The onset of a tone unit may be high or low; a high onset creates an extra center of attention. (See Section 11.3.)

When an utterance consists of two or more tone units, we can distinguish a nuclear tone unit, preceded by an onset tone unit and/or followed by a coda tone unit. Either of these may have a rise or a fall, with different effects for the whole utterance. (See Section 11.4.)

11.1 Paralanguage

The meanings which most of us think about, most of the time, are the meanings expressed in language. But there are more subtle meanings that are communicated in a speech situation. If two strangers who speak the same language have occasion to converse for a while and then go their separate ways, each will have some impression of the other: place of origin perhaps, social status, education, maybe something of the individual's personality (friendly, nervous, self-assured, restrained, etc.) and mood at the moment (tired, elated, angry, distraught, etc.), and the individual's attitude toward the context of this conversation and to the other participant. Part of these impressions is communicated by the words the speaker uses, the way they are pronounced, and the ways that words are put together to make utterances. All this is the primary channel of communication, what is vocal and verbal, the voice using words. Other meanings are communicated by elements that are neither vocal nor verbal: the distance maintained between the people in the conversation (the study and description of which is sometimes called **proxemics**); their posture, clothing, facial expressions, hair styles, and everything that can be called **appearance**; **gestures** made with head, arms, hands, or whole body – all the things which together are sometimes called 'body language.'

Some of the impressions are communicated by elements that are vocal but not verbal: the quality of the voice (as individual as our fingerprints), the relative loudness or softness, high or low pitch of the voice, the modulations of pitch from a near monotone to an exaggerated rising and falling, an unusually nasal or hoarse or rasping voice. These ways of using the voice while speaking are called **paralanguage**. The term paralanguage means 'alongside language,' therefore not part of the language system. Other vocal, non-verbal elements are part of language – the intonation system of the language.

QUESTIONS 11.1

We have certain conventional signals made with the voice that are not part of language and yet are probably known to all – or a large part – of those who speak English. Six of them appear below in their usual orthographic form, which does not represent the sounds very accurately.

(a) ps-st
(b) sh-sh
(c) huh
(d) unh-hunh
(e) br-r-r
(f) tsk-tsk

(The one labeled (e) is actually a labial trill, a sound made by keeping the lips slightly lax and letting them flutter in response to air exiting from the mouth; (f) is an apical or laminal click, produced by creating a vacuum in the mouth while the tongue is against the alveolar ridge, then releasing the tongue so that air rushes into the mouth from outside.)

What meaning do you attach to each of these? Is there a (more or less) standard gesture that has the same meaning as any of these – one that could be used to achieve the same effect visually instead of audibly? Is there a single word or a single utterance that expresses essentially what each of these vocal gestures conveys?

EXHIBIT 11.1 Linguistic and paralinguistic communication

Linguistic

Vocal and verbal	words in utterances
Vocal and nonverbal	prosody: accent and intonation
Nonvocal and verbal	signing; writing

Paralinguistic

Vocal	vocal gestures
	laughing, weeping, whisper, falsetto, tremolo
	relative loudness, relative pitch and pitch range, relative tempo, nasality, rasping
Nonvocal	gestures, posture, facial expression proximity
	appearance, clothing, cosmetics, jewelry, hair style

11.2 Intonations of the simple tone unit

If intonation is a system, it must have elements that contrast with one another. If it is a linguistic system, all speakers of the language must produce the same elements and recognize them when produced by others, and the elements – or patterns formed by the elements – must be capable of signaling contrasts of meaning.

The elements of intonation are changes of pitch. Pitch refers, of course, to frequency of vibration – of the vocal cords and therefore of the voiced sounds in speech. Since children have higher-pitched voices than adults and women have higher voices than men, pitch in intonation is a relative matter, not vibrations that can be described mathematically, like the vibrations of piano strings. So, when we say that some syllable is spoken with a high pitch, it means that the speaker's vocal cords are vibrating rapidly, for that person, and low pitch means slow vibration, within that individual's range. Rising and falling pitch indicate increasing and decreasing velocity, respectively.

The intonational elements recognized here are: long fall, short fall, long rise, short rise, fall–rise, and rise–fall.

If you have something to tell someone, you say it, you have no intention of saying anything more, you don't mean to imply more than you have said, and you don't expect a response, you will probably deliver the message with a **long fall** (↓) on the accented word, as in:

I think it's going to ↓ rain.

Here the change of pitch occurs completely in the word rain. Similarly, you might say, in a very definite way, "↓Yes" or "↓Certainly." If pitch changes on a single syllable, like *rain* or *Yes*, the voice 'glides down' – the change of vibration occurs on all the voiced elements of the syllable. For a polysyllabic word like *Certainly* the voice 'steps down' – the stressed syllable is high and the following one(s) low.

```
 r      Y      Cer
  ai      e
   n       s        tainly
```

We assume here that the long fall is the normal or 'unmarked' intonation. It is natural that vibration of the vocal cords will decrease as the speaker moves to the end of an utterance. With this assumption, other intonations have some special purpose; they are 'marked.'

Suppose that, instead of saying *Yes* in this deliberate way, you say that word in a rather abrupt manner, employing a **short fall** (for which we use the symbol ↘) as the voice fades away quickly: "↘Yes."

Whoever hears you may get the impression that you are busy, don't want to be bothered, or something of the sort. Suppose, as another example, you say "I think it's going to rain . . . " but intend to keep talking; *rain* will probably be spoken with a short fall.

```
↘Yés        . . .↘ráin
      Y              r
         es            ain
```

This intonation may be used in making a brief announcement to someone who is close ("I've ↘gót it").

The most obvious use of a **long rise** (↑) is in asking a yes–no question, that is, a question that does not begin with a question word (*Who, What, Where, When, Why, How*) and can be answered with *Yes* or *No*. One kind of question has the word order of a statement but is spoken with a rising tune instead of a falling one.

This is a ↑jóke?

A more common sort of question is made with inversion – putting a verb in first place.

Is this a ↑jóke?

Since inverted word order marks this utterance as a question, the rising tune is redundant, and thus a falling tune is possible.

Is this a ↓jóke?

Next, consider these questions that contain a question word:

You're leaving ↑whén?
She left it ↑whére?
They couldn't find ↑whát?
↑Whó couldn't find the answer?

These utterances are marked as questions by the inclusion of a question word. The question word appears in the same position in the sentence as the answer would appear – at the beginning if the question word is subject, after the verb if it is not. The question word is the accented word, the place where the voice rises.

Do you think it's going to ↑ráin?   Are you ↑súre?

Here the accented syllable may begin high and continue rising (that is, accelerating) or begin low and rise to a high pitch. There seems to be no difference of meaning attached to these slight intonational differences.

```
              e                          e
          sur                          r
   Are you                  Are you   u
                                      s
```

Another contrast is seen in utterances that begin with a question word:

Where will the meeting be ↓héld?   ↓Whére?
↑Whére will the meeting be held?   ↑Whére?

A falling intonation is common in such WH-questions – those that begin with a question word – when the speaker is seeking information about something that has not yet been communicated, at least not to the speaker. The rising intonation is used when the speaker is asking for repetition or clarification of something already said. In this example the question might be paraphrased as "I know the meeting place was mentioned but I missed that information" or " . . . but I'm not sure" or " . . . but I can't believe what I've heard."

A long rise may be used in contradicting. If a child says, for example, "I'm not going to eat my ↓spínach," his mother might very well respond "Oh yes you ↑áre."

Just as a short fall is used for brief utterances between people occupying the same small area, a **short rise** can be the way in which we try to attract someone's attention ("↗Máry") or of responding when another person tries to get our attention ("↗Yés?"). "↑Óh?" with a long rise expresses surprise at what has been said; "↗Óh" with a short rise is only an expression of interest.

In the **fall–rise** intonation (indicated here with ˇ) the accented syllable has high tone, after which the voice falls and then rises slightly. One use of the fall–rise is to express agreement but reservation.

```
   Y                c
      s.      You an        that way.
   e                do it
```

"ˇYés" is somewhat equivalent to saying "That's true, but . . . "; "You ˇcán do it that way" implies something like " . . . but I don't think you should." "I supˇpóse that's ríght" is quite far removed from "That's ↓ ríght." A fall–rise can reinforce an accent used for paradigmatic focus: "Have ↑you got any? | ˇÍ haven't."

Some speakers use the fall–rise in short formulas of politeness or leave-taking.

ˇThánk you.
You're ˇwélcome.
See you toˇmórrow.

A **rise–fall** intonation (shown with ^) is a more dynamic or more dramatic equivalent of a simple long fall. You might, for example, say "^Éxcellent" or "That's ^wónderful" to express your feelings in a forceful way. You might, as another example, say "It's going to ^ráin" when repeating this message to someone who didn't understand you the first time or perhaps didn't seem to be suitably impressed by what you had to say.

```
      on            a
  w   der       r i
        ful          n
```

To summarize, we have considered six intonations or intonational contours and have illustrated them in situations, and with speaker intentions, that should be familiar to readers of this book. It would be wrong, however, to give the impression that any of these intonations has a clear, limited meaning or that any meaning can be expressed only with a specific intonation. In general, we see that a falling contour indicates finality (in a statement); it can be used in a WH-question, which carries a presupposition ("Where will the meeting be ↓héld?" presupposes that a meeting will be held somewhere); it is possible in a yes–no question ("Can this really be ↓trúe?") though this may give the impression that the speaker is not actually asking for information; and the long fall may occur in a command ("Put the books a↓wáy now"). Clearly it is the most-used intonation, and our real task is to explain the other contours.

A short fall indicates finality that is not complete; it may occur in short utterances of a commonplace nature, where the message would probably be clear from the situation. Unless it is followed by another utterance, it may suggest brusqueness or indifference, but that depends on what the addressee expects.

A rise–fall is an emphatic kind of long fall.

A long rise is oriented toward the person addressed. It seeks information (in the yes–no question) or contradicts what was said previously.

A short rise is also addressee-oriented. Unless the speaker follows up with another utterance, it indicates a show of interest, of waiting to hear from the addressee.

A fall–rise suggests agreement but reservation; what the addressee has just said is true but not the whole truth; it occurs with paradigmatic contrast ("He didn't tell me ˇthát" is more or less equivalent to "He told me something but not that").

These intonations differ, then, in the general effects that they have but their interpretation, meaning, depends on the context in which the utterance occurs, just as the meanings of words vary with context.

QUESTIONS 11.2

1 Does the utterance "Yes, it is" differ in these contexts? If so, how?

Is Bangkok in Thailand?   Yes, it is.
Bangkok's not in Thailand.   Yes, it is.

2 Does "When?" differ in these contexts? If so, how?

Your flight boards at for-forf.   When? (didn't get the message)
Your flight boards at Gate 9.   When?

3 You ask the same question of three people. They all give you the same verbal response but with different intonations. How do you interpret their answers?

Have you heard about my latest fishing trip?
ˆNo. ˇNo. ˋNo.

11.3 Low and high onsets

The intonations discussed above take place from the accented syllable – the nucleus – to the end of the tone unit. We should now note how a high pitch in the onset of the tone unit can give what is said an extra focus, in addition to the focus signaled by the nucleus, or extend the focus signaled by the nucleus. Suppose someone you know well tells you he or she is going to a wedding. Depending on how much interest this fact arouses in you, you might say either of these:

```
              má              Who's        má
Who's getting              getting
           rried?                         rried?
```

The first of these has a low (or non-high) onset, the second one a high onset, which indicates that the speaker is – or wants to seem – very much interested. We indicate the high onset with a small circle: "°Who's getting ↓márried?"

Another contrastive example, first with low onset, then with high onset.

```
                              hó
I've looked in every room in the   u
                                     se.

              every room in the hó
I've looked in                   u
                                  se.
```

The second utterance, with high onset, does not communicate any more than the first utterance about what the speaker has done; it adds emphasis by highlighting the expression *every room*.

Words with emotional connotations – expressing favorable or unfavorable attitudes – may have a high onset and a low fall.

(a)   She seems like a °very nice ↘gírl.
(b)   I'm sure we'll be °quite ↘háppy here.
(c)   I °really wish I could ↘dó that.

Social formulas that are frequently used may have a high onset with a short fall or a fall–rise on the accented word.

°That's ⌄ríght.   °O⌄káy.   °O˅káy.   °Good˅níght.

This intonation, with the short fall, is often used in WH-questions ("°How do you ⌄feel today?") and it may occur in commands ("°Just wait a ⌄mínute"); with a short or long rise it is frequent in yes–no questions ("°Are you ↑góing now?").

One might say "I'm sorry" when asking another person to repeat – somewhat more polite than "What did you say?" The utterance would probably be "I'm ↑sórry." How would you say "I'm sorry" when you need to interrupt two people who are conversing? How would you say "I'm sorry" when you accidentally bump into someone?

11.4 Compound tunes

An utterance, as we know, can consist of more than one tone unit. One of them is the nuclear tone unit and others form the onset and/or the coda. Exhibit 11.2 illustrates some fairly simple utterances.

EXHIBIT 11.2 Utterance structure

Onset	Nucleus	Coda
	The food is good.	
The food is good ǀ	and the prices are reasonable.	
They've been here ǀ	about a month, ǀ	haven't they?

We first consider sequences of onset + nuclear tone unit. An onset tone unit typically has a short fall, a short rise, or a fall–rise. The rise or fall–rise on an introductory phrase or clause establishes a frame for what follows.

(a)   Later ↗ón, | we might have a game of ↓chéss.
(b)   If I go ˇhóme, | I won't be back before ↓thrée.

The short fall is neutral. When a long utterance is broken up or when the speaker wants to emphasize more than one word in the utterance, onset tone units have short falls.

(a)   Your ↘fríend | isn't ↓hére yet.
(b)   I thought the ↘book | was better than the ˇmovie.
(c)   The bus is ↘chéap enough, | but a ↘táxi | would be fáster.

Enumerating a series of items can be done with short falls or short rises on all items except the last, which has a long fall.

(a)   ↘Óne | ↘twó | ↘thrée | ↘fóur | ↓fíve.
(b)   ↗Óne | ↗twó | ↗thrée | ↗fóur | ↓fíve.

Questions that present two or more alternatives have a long rise in each tone unit except the last, which has a long fall.

(a)   Shall we go by ↑bús | or by ↓tráin?
(b)   Do your prefer the ↑blúe one | or the ↑púrple | or ↓néither?
(c)   Is your son in the ↑Ármy | or the ↓Návy?

Alternative questions like these carry a sort of presupposition that all possible answers are contained in the question – which of course need not be true. Compare (d) with (c) above:

(d)   Is your son in the Army or the ↑Návy?

This is a yes–no question, which has a different sort of presupposition: namely, that the answer is either "Yes" (he is in one of the two) or "No" (he is not in either the Army or the Navy).

    Now we turn to the sequence of nuclear tone unit + coda. After a long fall (from high to low) in the nuclear tone unit, a tag comment may continue at the low level, shown here with the symbol → on the accented syllable.

(a)   You're °absolutely ↓wróng | in →fáct.
(b)   ↓Nó, un→fórtunately.
(c)   ↓Whát, for ex→ample?
(d)   You can do it ↓thát way, | if you →wánt to.

Instead of the low continuation, a low rise on the tag comment seems more oriented toward the addressee; it is likely to be interpreted as more friendly or more polite.

You can do it ↓thát way, | if you ↗wánt to.

Similarly, a tag vocative may continue at low level or have a short rise. "Good ↓mórning, | →sír" is apt to sound routine, polite, even submissive. "Good ↓mórning, | ↗sír" would seem to come from someone who is bright and eager. Other examples:

(a)   Good ↘mórning, | Miss ↗Smíth.
(b)   ↓Yés, | ↗déar.
(c)   We're ↓cóunting on you, | ↗Hárry.

After a nuclear tone unit with a long rise (from low to high), the tag comment or vocative continues at a high level.

(a)   Will there be time for a ↑chéss game, | in →thát case?
(b)   Are your ready to ↑gó, | →Jím?

Tag questions are common in English and troublesome for the foreigner learning the language. Whereas some languages get along nicely with a simple *n'est-ce pas?* or *nicht wahr?* attached to a statement to ask about the truth of that statement, English requires a form of *be* or an auxilairy (*have, do, will, would, can, could, shall, should, may, might, must*) and a personal pronoun or the pseudo-pronoun *there*. A negative tag is common after an affirmative statement ("There's a game scheduled for today, isn't there?") and an affirmative tag after a negative statement ("It's not time to go, is it?"). Compare falling (usually short fall) and rising (usually short rise) intonations.

(a)   You a↘gree with me, | ↘dón't you?
(b)   You a↘gree with me, | ↗dón't you?

With the falling intonation the speaker is not asking for information but rather seeking confirmation on what he or she believes. In this case, an affirmative answer is expected. The rising intonation, in contrast, is oriented toward the addressee. The speaker has no definite expectation. An affirmative statement can be followed by an affirmative tag, as in:

You be↘lieve that, | ↘dó you?

A falling intonation is probable because the utterance is closer to being a comment than a true question.

EXHIBIT 11.3 Miscellaneous intonational contrasts ━━━━━━━━━

(a) Who ↓phóned this afternoon, | ↗Fránk?
(b) Who ↓phóned this afternoon? | ↑Fránk?

((a) a question directed to Frank; (b) two questions)

(c) This is my ↓síster, | ↗Ánnie.
(d) This is my ↘síster, | ↓Annie.

((c) a statement directed to Annie; (d) an identification)

(e) Do you want to see the ↑hóckey game | or the ↓pláy?
(f) Do you want to see a ↑hóckey game? | Or a ↑pláy?

((e) two choices offered; (f) two separate questions)

(g) ↑Whát did you say?
(h) What did you ↓sáy?

((g) a request for a repetition; (h) a possible response to an utterance like "I spoke to the manager this afternoon.")

(i) Put these things a↓wáy.
(j) °Put these things a↘wáy.

((i) a possible answer to "What are you going to do?"; (j) clearly an order to someone else)

(k) °Why don't you ask ↓Hárris?
(l) Why don't you ask ↓Hárris?

((k) a question that is really a suggestion; (l) a true question)

(m)   I ˅líke it.
(n)   °I ˅líke it.
(o)   I ˇlike it.

((m) a plain statement; (n) an enthusiastic statement; (o) a statement with reservation)

(p)   ↓Cáll me | if you need →hélp.
(q)   ↓Cáll me | if you need ↗hélp.

(Which speaker gives the impression of being more willing to help?)

EXHIBIT 11.4   Tone units as onsets and as codas

An introductory word, phrase, or clause in the onset is likely to have a low rise or fall–rise; the same forms, when they occur as coda, typically are spoken with low level or low rise.

1   (a)   If it doesn't ↗ráin, | we'll play ˅ténnis.
      (b)   We'll play ˅ténnis, | if it doesn't ↗ráin.
2   (a)   As a matter of ↗fáct, | that's °not quite what I ˩méant.
      (b)   That's °not quite what I ˇméant, | as a matter of →fáct.
3   (a)   How˘éver, | there's bound to be a˩nóther opportunity | ˩láter.
      (b)   There's bound to be a˩nóther opportunity | ˩láter, | how→ever.
4   (a)   In ˇthát case, | we should expect a decision °fairly ˩sóon.
      (b)   We should expect a decision °fairly ˩sóon, | in ↗thát case.

PRACTICE 11.4

Mark the following utterances with appropriate tone marks.

1 The bus goes to Clifton, Avonlea, Holly, and Fox Hill.
2 Can you do me a favor? Maybe.
3 We had a great time there.
4 To tell the truth, I'm not at all impressed.
5 Did you know she's won three gold medals? Three?

LOOKING BACK

A spoken utterance consists of words put together in a grammatical construction; this part is verbal and vocal. While people are producing such utterances, they are also communicating something, intentionally or not, by elements that are not part of language, neither vocal nor verbal, such as gestures, appearance, stance, and proximity to the addressees – popularly called body language, labeled kinesics by those who study such things systematically. This chapter has been about elements in speech apart from pronunciation of words, elements that are vocal but not verbal. Some of these elements may be considered vocal gestures that accompany speech: laughing, giggling, whispering, falsetto, a quavering or 'breaking' voice. Some are individual ways of speaking: some people are louder than others, or louder at certain times; some have higher-pitched voices than others; some speak in a near monotone while others have a broad pitch range; some clip syllables short by comparison with others who drawl. These and other such phenomena are part of speech but not part of language.

Intonation is vocal, non-verbal, and part of language. It is the use of (relative) pitch changes in patterns used and recognized by all speakers of a language (allowing for dialect differences analogous to other phonological and semantic differences) and which can impart different meanings to otherwise identical utterances.

The elements of intonation are changes of pitch associated with the accented syllable of the tone unit. In single tone units we have recognized a long fall, a short fall, a long rise, a short rise, a rise–fall, and a fall–rise. In describing the meanings expressed (or expressible) by these intonations we perhaps need to make clear that contrasts can be made by intonation alone but that different intonations do not necessarily create a difference of meaning, nor is there always a single way of making a difference.

In general, a falling tune suggests finality and may suggest that the speaker is fully confident of his or her utterance and/or of the reply he or she will receive. A short fall is a more abrupt termination than a long fall. The rise–fall is more intense than a simple fall. Rising tunes are listener-oriented, indicate the speaker's desire for a reply (not an expectation), or may be used to refute what the interlocutor has previously said. A fall–rise intensifies a contrast in the discourse and is often used to suggest that something more might be said.

Greater intensity may be expressed in a tone unit by high pitch in the onset of the tone unit.

In an utterance composed of several tone units – a compound contour – we may recognize a nuclear tone unit preceded by one or more tone units that make up the onset of the utterance and/or tone units that constitute the coda. An onset tone unit has a short fall if it is preliminary/introductory with respect to the nuclear tone unit, a short rise if it establishes an antithesis. A sequence of onset tone units, rising or falling, is the listing intonation. A coda tone unit is a tag, level at low or high level or else rising; it contains a vocative, a question, or a commentary.

Suggested readings

A different – and deeper – investigation of the borderline between paralanguage and intonation will be found in Crystal (1969). Chapter 3 is especially recommended.

To date, there has been no thorough investigation of dialect differences in intonation throughout the English-speaking world. Cruttenden (1986: Chapter 5) contains more information on this subject than any other work.

Notes

Apart from the two books mentioned above, the following will be useful to anyone who wants to acquire a better understanding of intonation: Pike (1945), Kingdon (1958b), Halliday (1967), O'Connor and Arnold (1973), Brown, Currie, and Kenworthy (1980), Bing (1985), Bolinger (1986), Couper-Kuhlen (1986), and Pierrehumbert (1987).

Lyons (1995) uses the term 'paralanguage' to include visual phenomena – gestures, stance, appearance, proximity – as well as vocal features that are not intonational. The usual practice is to restrict the term only to vocal, non-verbal phenomena, but there is clearly a need for a term that includes both the visual and the vocal.

Chapter 12

Morphemes that vary in form

- **12.1 Phonologically conditioned alternations** 197
- **12.2 Morphological conditioning** 200
- **12.3 Another past tense suffix** 206

LOOKING AHEAD

Some morphemes have more than one phonological form; for example, *give* has a different form *gif-* before /t/ in *gift*; the final consonant of *north*, /θ/, changes to /ð/ in *north-ern*; in *south*, *south-ern* there is the same change in the final consonant and also a vowel change; compare *east*, *east-ern* and *west*, *west-ern* with no change. The different forms are called the allomorphs of the morpheme. In some instances the alternation depends on phonological factors – the difference is due to a difference of stress, of neighboring phonemes (as in *gift*), or of position in a word. Such alternations are said to be **phonologically conditioned**. Other alternations, like that in *north*, cannot be explained by phonological facts. These variations are due to changes that took place in the earlier history of English or in languages from which English has acquired a large part of its vocabulary. In today's English, to tell which allomorph occurs in what context, we have to state the context in terms of neighboring morphemes. These alternations are **morphologically conditioned**. Section 12.1 describes some phonologically conditioned alternations that are already partly familiar to you: assimilation (including palatalization), consonant cluster reduction, and vowel reduction. Section 12.2 takes up alternations that are morphologically conditioned or partly phonological and partly morphological. These are called spirantization, velar softening, voice alternation, and free vowel/checked vowel alternation.

Phonologically conditioned alternations are easy to understand and describe; we can call one allomorph the basic one and show that the other allomorph is derived from it. In other instances there is no good reason for deriving either allomorph from the other. Instead we can establish an abstract form from which both are derived. Such abstract forms are considered in Section 12.3.

12.1 Phonologically conditioned alternations

This section deals with four kinds of morpheme variation that have a phonological basis: assimilation, palatalization, consonant cluster reduction, and vowel reduction.

One kind of phonologically conditioned variation is assimilation. We are already familiar with this process at word boundaries, as in *can go* and *is she*, where a word-final phoneme takes on some feature of the following word-initial phoneme. Assimilation is seen also in the negative prefix *in-*, which becomes *im-* before a labial consonant:

indecent intangible improper imbalance

Examples of palatalization are especially common. When a morpheme that ends with /t d s z/ is followed by a morpheme that begins with /j/, the result is /č ǰ ʃ ʒ/, respectively. Note what happens when *-ure*, /jər/, is added to *depart*, *proceed*, *press*, *compose*, ending, respectively, with /t d s z/; the results are *departure*, *procedure*, *pressure*, *composure*, with /č ǰ ʃ ʒ/, respectively. More examples of palatalization are found in Exhibit 12.1.

Chapter 7 included discussion of consonant cluster simplification, such as the loss of /t/ in *don't know*. Here is a different kind of cluster simplification:

column-ist damn-ation hymn-al solemn-ize
column   damn   hymn   solemn

Each morpheme ends with /mn/ when another morpheme with initial vowel follows. But English words do not end with two nasal consonants (Chapter 6), so the phoneme /n/ is deleted in final position, even though our spelling conventions maintain final *-mn*. (However, note *damning*, where the suffix is an inflection. The allomorph that occurs before the inflection is the same as the one that occurs in final position.)

Deleting a consonant is one way of resolving a consonant cluster that cannot occur in word-final position. Another method of doing the same thing is to insert a vowel between consonants. Let's look at these examples:

angr-y	centr-al	diametr-ic	entr-ance	monstr-ous
anger	center	diameter	enter	monster

EXHIBIT 12.1 Alternations due to palatalization ━━━━━━━━━

/t/	/č/	/d/	/ǰ/
cult	culture	fraud	fraudulent
depart	departure	grand	grandeur
moist	moisture	proceed	procedure
sculptor	sculpture	gradient	gradual
digest	digestion		
exhaust	exhaustion		
act	actual		
habit	habitual		
contempt	contemptuous		
event	eventual		

/s/	/ʃ/	/z/	/ʒ/
coerce	coercion	compose	composure
press	pressure	disclose	disclosure
sense	sensual	infuse	infusion
sex	sexual	please	pleasure
commerce	commercial	revise	revision
face	facial	seize	seizure
malice	malicious		

When we cut away the suffixes *-y*, *-al*, *-ic*, *-ance*, *-ous*, we find base morphemes that end with an obstruent consonant plus /r/. English words may end with a sequence of sonorant consonant plus obstruent consonant, but not a sequence of obstruent consonant plus sonorant consonant, like /gr/ and /tr/. So in final position /ə/ is inserted between /t/ and /r/ – or, putting it another way, /r/ is changed to /ə(r)/. (Note again that the allomorph in final position is also the one that occurs before inflections, e.g. *centered*, *entering*.)

Words like the following, which have the same base morpheme with and without a suffix, or with different suffixes, are stressed on different syllables.

átom	atóm-ic
Ítaly	Itáli-an
ecónom-y	èconóm-ic

órigin	orígin-al
pólitic-s	polític-al

Comparing the first vowel of *atom* and the first vowel of *atomic*, we see that a stressed /æ/ is 'reduced' to /ə/ in an unstressed syllable; comparing the second vowel of *atomic* with the second vowel of *atom* shows a stressed /ɒ/ reduced to an unstressed /ə/. Comparing stressed vowels with their unstressed counterparts in the remaining words leads to a similar, general conclusion: a checked vowel in a stressed (or strong) syllable becomes /ə/ or /ɪ/ when that syllable is unstressed.

In words like these – roughly, words of Latin and Greek origin – the spelling of a morpheme represents, not a single pronunciation, but two or more pronunciations. How do you pronounce *atom-*, *Ital-*, *econom-*, *origin-*, *politic-*? That depends on what, if anything, follows. The spelling represents something abstract. It has no pronunciation in itself until stress is assigned (according to the stress rules of Chapter 8) to whole words. Then vowel phonemes are 'assigned' to vowel letters. We might represent the assignments of stress and phonemes in the five pairs of words this way:

	atom	atom-ic	itali	itali-an
Stress assignment	´	´	´	´
Vowel assignment	ǽ ə	ə ɒ́ ɪ	ɪ´ə i	ɪ ǽ j ə
Result	ǽtəm	ətɒ́mɪk	ítəli	ɪtǽljən

	econom-y	econom-ic	origin	original
Stress assignment	´	` ´	´	´
Vowel assignment	ɪ ɒ ə i	ɛ̀ ə ɒ́ ɪ	ɔ ə ɪ	ə ʃ ə ə
Result	ɪkɒ́nəm i	ɛ̀kənɒ́m ɪk	ɔrəjɪn	ɔrʃjənəl

PROBLEM 12.1

Compare the pronunciation – the phonological form – of these words:

fiddle   juggle   peddle

with these

fiddler   juggler   peddler

Each of the three morphemes has two allomorphs. What are they? What is inserted in one allomorph to produce the other? Why?

12.2 Morphological conditioning

Consider the words *democrat*, *democrat-ic*, and *democrac-y* and the words *anesthet-ic*, *anesthet-ist*, *anesthes-ia*. There is an alternation of /t/ and /s/ in these forms but the alternation cannot be explained in phonological terms. Examining more data will show that /s/ occurs before the noun ending /-i/ (spelled with Y), as in *democracy*; before the ending *-is* as in *analysis*; and before /i/ followed by another vowel, as in *anesthesia*; /t/ is usual in final position, before the suffix *-ic(al)*, and in most other positions. The alternation of /t/ and /s/ – or the change of /t/ to /s/ – has the traditional name spirantization; more examples appear in Exhibit 12.2.

Consider the words *president*, *presidency*, *presidential*. The first has the final consonant /t/; the second shows spirantization, a change to /s/ before *-y*; the third word has /ʃ/, which results from palatalization of /s/ before /i/ plus another vowel, just like *compress*, *compression* or *malice*, *malicious*. Two 'rules' apply before /i/ and another vowel: spirantization changes /t/ to /s/; then palatalization changes /s/ to /ʃ/. A pair of words like *part*, *partial* or *relate*, *relation* shows alternation of /t/ and /ʃ/. We can consider these also as examples of spirantization and palatalization, even though there is no intermediate example of /s/. English has numerous verb–noun pairs like *relate*, *relation*; *corrupt*, *corruption*; *except*, *exception*. Exhibit 12.3 has more examples.

EXHIBIT 12.2 Alternation of /t/ and /s/ in words of Greek and Latin origin ━━━━━━━━━

analytic, paralytic	analysis, paralysis
anesthetic, anesthetist	anesthesia
cathartic	catharsis
democratic	democracy
hyocrite	hypocrisy
ecstatic	ecstasy
genetic	genesis
epileptic	epilepsy
synoptic	synopsis
dyspeptic	dyspepsia
emphatic	emphasis, emphasize
prophet, prophetic	prophesy, prophecy
metropolitan	metropolis
hemostat	hemostasis

parenthetical	parentheses
synthetic	synthesis
galactic /-kt-/	galaxy /-ks-/
diagnostic /-st-/	diagnosis /-st- → -s-/
confederate	confederacy
delicate	delicacy
literate	literacy
pirate	piracy
secret	secrecy
frequent	frequency
hesitant	hesitancy
infant	infancy
vacant	vacancy

EXHIBIT 12.3 Alternation of /t/ and /s/ and /ʃ/

/t/	/s/	/ʃ/
resident	residence	residential
act		action
exempt		exemption
part		partial
permit	permissive	permission

The next alternation to consider also has a traditional name, velar softening. It has two parts: one is the alternation of /k/ and /s/; the other is the alternation of /g/ and /ǰ/. The first is exemplified in *critic, critic-al, critic-ize, critic-ism*. Our writing system uses the letter C to represent both phonemes; that letter represents /s/ when the next letter is E, I, or Y; it represents /k/ when it is word-final, followed by A, O, U, or a consonant.

In *electric(-al), electric-ity, electric-ian* two changes occur. Velar softening is responsible for the change from /k/ to /s/, and palatalization is responsible for the change from /s/ to /ʃ/. In *music, musician* the same two changes occur, leading from /k/ in *music* to /ʃ/ in *musician*. However, there is no intermediate word with /s/. More examples of these alternations are in Exhibit 12.4.

The words *analogue, analog-ous, analog-y* exemplify the alternation of /g/ and /ǰ/. Here too our writing system uses one letter, G, to represent both phonemes. G stands for /ǰ/ before E, I, and Y, and for /g/ elsewhere – though there are numerous irregularities. Exhibit 12.5 contains other examples of /g/ alternating with /ǰ/ and also a few examples of /g/ changing to /k/ before a voiceless consonant. Alternation of a voiced obstruent with the corresponding voiceless obstruent, and vice versa, is the next alternation to be examined.

EXHIBIT 12.4 Alternation of /k/ and /s/ (and /ʃ/)

/k/	/s/	/ʃ/
electric	electricity	electrician
magic		magician
Patrick		Patricia
critical	criticize	
elastic	elasticity	
medical	medicine	
romantic	romanticism	
reciprocal	reciprocity	
mathematical		mathematician

EXHIBIT 12.5 Alternation of /g/, /ǰ/, and /k/

/g/	/ǰ/	/k/
legal	legislate	
analogous	analogy	
fragment	fragile	fracture
legal	legitimate	
laryngoscope	laryngitis	larynx
pedagogue	pedagogy	
pragmatic		practice

The word *give* ends with /v/; in *gif-t* /v/ changes to /f/ before the following voiceless consonant. We see the same change in *twelve* and *twelf-th*. If we take /v/ as the 'basic' phoneme, the change to /f/ before a voiceless consonant is phonologically conditioned. On the other hand, if we were to consider /f/ the basic phoneme, there is no phonological reason for /f/ to become /v/ in word-final position since English words end with both voiceless and voiced consonants.

In *wolf* and the plural *wolves*, in the noun *grief* and the verb *grieve*, in the noun *mischief* and the adjective *mischievous* the same alternation of /f/ and /v/ occurs without any phonological reason – in Modern English. The alternation is due to conditions that existed at an earlier stage of the language when [v] occurred only between voiced phonemes and the 'silent E' of *wolves* and *grieve* was not 'silent.'

A similar alternation is that of /θ/ and /ð/ in *north, northern* and *south, southern,* examples that began this chapter. Likewise, /s/ and /z/ are seen alternating in the nouns *house* and *excuse* versus the verbs *house* and *excuse*. At one time voiced fricatives occurred only between voiced phonemes and the voiceless fricatives occurred elsewhere. When these phonological conditions changed, voiceless and voiced fricatives came to be contrasting phonemes in the same positions of occurrence, but the alternation of these fricatives still remains in certain morphemes. All three of these voiced–voiceless pairs are illustrated in Exhibit 12.6.

EXHIBIT 12.6 Alternation in voice

/f/ and /v/ *calf, calves* (pl.), *calve* (v.)

> bereave, bereft; half, halves, halve; elf, elves; grief, grieve; leaf, leaves; life, lives, lively; loaf, loaves; mischief, mischievous; proof, prove; relief, relieve; shelf, shelves, shelve; strife, strive; twelfth, twelve

/θ/ and /ð/ *cloth, clothe, clothing*

> bath, bathe; breath, breathe; mouth (n.), mouth (v.); north, northerly; south, southerly; teeth, teethe; worth, worthy; wreath, wreathe

/s/ and /z/ *house, houses* (pl.), *house* (v.)

> abuse (n.), abuse (v.); advice, advise; excuse (n.), excuse (v.); glass, glaze; grass, graze; grease, greasy; use (n.), use (v.)

(Some speakers have /s/ rather than /z/ in *houses*; many speakers have /s/ in *greasy*.)

There are numerous morphemes that show an alternation in vowels, in addition to those in which the alternation accompanies a shift in word stress, as in *atom, atomic*. For example, *south, southern* shows an alternation of /au/ and /ʌ/ as well as the alternation of /θ/ and /ð/. The same vowel alternation is seen in *pronounce, pronunciation* and *abound, abundant*, in all cases an alternation of vowels in the nuclear syllable.

Some of the most common vowel alternations are the five illustrated below, free vowels alternating with certain checked vowels:

/ei/, /æ/	insane, insan-ity; volcan-o, volcan-ic
/ii/, /ɛ/	deep, dep-th; extreme, extrem-ity
/ai/, /ɪ/	wide, wid-th; divine, divin-ity
/ou/, /ɒ/	cone, con-ical; sole, sol-itude
/(j)uu/, /ʌ/	produce, produc-tive; duke, duchess

Our school tradition calls vowel phonemes by the names of vowel letters: /ei/ is 'long A' and /æ/ is 'short A'; /ii/ and /ɛ/ are 'long E' and 'short E,' respectively; /ai/ and /ɪ/ are 'long and short I'; /ou/ and /ɒ/ are 'long and short O'; /juu/ and /ʌ/ are 'long and short U.' (Of course, there are other spellings for these phonemes; for example, 'long A' also has the spelling AI, as in *vain*, and EI, as in *vein*.) These names would not make much sense if they were meant to describe the pronunciations of today. They actually refer to pronunciations of the thirteenth century and earlier. Seven centuries ago the nuclear vowel of *insane* was like the nuclear vowel of *insanity* but longer, the vowel of *deep* was a lengthened version of the vowel in *depth*, the vowel of *wide* the lengthened equivalent of the vowel in *width*, and so forth. Later, the long vowels underwent a change and became quite different from the short vowels which they once matched in sound. They still 'match' but only as alternates in a number of morphemes.

This alternation occurs in some contexts that cannot be explained phonologically: *Spain, Spanish*; *zeal, zealous*; *final, finish*; *clothe, cloth*. On the other hand, the checked vowel is usual when two or more consonants follow and when two or more syllables follow in the same word. Exhibit 12.7 presents examples of alternations with these two factors, and also alternation where the checked vowel occurs before a particular morpheme, the suffix *-ic*.

─────── **EXHIBIT 12.7** Free vowel/checked vowel alternation

1   The checked vowel occurs before a coda of two or more syllables:

    A: /ei/, /æ/ explain, explanatory; fable, fabulous; opaque, opacity;
sane, sanity; table, tabular
    E: /ii/, /ɛ/ compete, competitive; female, feminine; hero, heroine;
obscene, obscenity; supreme, supremacy
    I: /ai/, /ɪ/ crime, criminal; derive, derivative; mine, mineral; sublime,
sublimity; tyrant, tyranny
    O: /ou/, /ɒ/ code, codify; globe, globular; mediocre, mediocrity;
provoke, provocative; sole, solitude

2   The checked vowel occurs before two consonants:

    E: /ii/, /ɛ/ clean, cleanse; heal, health; redeem, redemption
    I: /ai/, /ɪ/ five, fifty; defile, filth; drive, drift; scribe, script
    O: /ou/, /ɒ/ nose, nostril
    U: /juu/, /ʌ/ produce, productive; consume, consumption

3   The checked vowel occurs before the coda -ic(al):

    A: /ei/, /æ/ volcano, volcanic
    E: /ii/, /ɛ/ athlete, athletic; meter, metric
    I: /ai/, /ɪ/ arthritis, arthritic; Bible, Biblical; cycle, cyclic; satire, satiric;
type, typical
    O: /ou/, /ɒ/ colon, colic; episode, episodic; neurosis, neurotic; micro-
scope, microscopic; telephone, telephonic

QUESTIONS 12.2

1 The words *completion*, *facial*, and *musician* all contain the
phoneme /ʃ/, which is the result of palatalization. However,
only one of these has an allomorph that results from palatalization alone. Explain.
2 The three words above illustrate another phenomenon: before
/ʃ/ A, E, O, and U represent free vowels; compare *facial*,
palatial, *vacation*; *completion*; *atrocious*, *promotion*; *pollution*.
But I stands for the checked vowel /ɪ/. What are the simple
words related to: *ignition*, *sufficient*, *vicious*?

12.3 Another past tense suffix

Chapter 6 contained an account of the regular past tense morpheme. As we saw, it has three regular allomorphs, /id/, /t/, and /d/. They are regular because each occurs in a particular phonological environment: /id/ after verbs that end with /t/ or /d/, /t/ after other voiceless phonemes, and /d/ after all other regular verbs, that is, after voiced phonemes other than /d/ itself. We can see that /d/ is the 'basic' allomorph; it occurs in the most environments and, furthermore, the other two allomorphs are the result of necessary adjustment: /d/ cannot occur after /d/ or /t/, so a vowel must be inserted; /d/ cannot occur after voiceless consonants, so it must assimilate and become /t/. Let's call this the /d/ suffix.

English has about a hundred verbs that are irregular in the formation of the past tense and past participle, such as *buy*, *bought*; *find*, *found*; *sing*, *sang*, *sung*. To describe these formations is clearly not a simple task. However, some of them are more regular than they might seem at first glance, if we keep in mind some of the alternations already examined in this chapter: consonant cluster simplification, assimilation, and the free vowel/checked vowel alternation.

1   Some verbs can have the regular ending /d/ for the past tense and past participle or they may have the ending /t/:

Simple form	*Past tense and past participle*
burn	burned *or* burnt
spill	spilled *or* spilt

Other verbs like these are:

learn smell spell spoil

So there is a /t/ suffix as well as a /d/ suffix for past tense and it occurs after this small group of verbs that have /n/ or /l/ as the final consonant.

burn + /d/ → burned
burn + /t/ → burnt

2   Now consider another small group of verbs:

Simple form	Past tense and past participle
bend	bent
build	built
lend	lent
send	sent
spend	spent

With this small group of verbs there is no alternative: the simple form of the verb ends in *-nd* or *-ld* and the past tense and past participle are formed by changing *-d* to *-t*. But our two groups really have the same suffix /t/. The second group requires a small adjustment when /t/ is added: /d/ is deleted.

    burn + /t/ → burnt
    bend + /t/ → bent

3   Now consider a third group:

Simple form	Past tense, past participle
bet	bet
spread	spread

The simple form, the past tense, and the past participle are identical; if we want to say that the past tense and past participle are made from the simple form (as with other verbs), then they are formed by adding zero. Here are others like *bet* and *spread*:

    burst cast (broadcast forecast) cost cut hit hurt knit let put quit rid set shed shut slit split sweat thrust wed set

You notice that these verbs all end in /d/ or /t/ preceded by a short vowel. Let's say that these verbs, too, have the suffix /t/, but when /t/ is added to /d/ or /t/, it appears as zero–cluster simplification.

    bet + /t/ → bet
    spread + /t/ → spread

Several of the verbs listed above have a regular past tense formation as well as having past tense identical with the simple form. For instance, the past tense of *knit* can be *knitted* as well as just *knit*.

We can say that these are manifestations of two different suffixes, /d/ and /t/.

> knit + /d/ → knitted
> knit + /t/ → knit

4   Our fourth group is composed of several sub-groups.

(a)

creep	crept	deal	dealt	dream	dreamt
keep	kept	feel	felt	mean	meant
sleep	slept				
sweep	swept	leave	left		
weep	wept				

All these verbs have the free vowel /ii/. They add the suffix /t/ and undergo another change: /ii/ is replaced by the checked vowel /ɛ/. In *leave* another change occurs, voicing assimilation: /v/ → /f/ before /t/.

> /kiip + t/ → /kɛpt/
> /fiil + t/ → /fɛlt/
> /liiv + t/ → /lɛft/

(b)

bleed	bled	meet	met
breed	bred		
feed	fed		
lead	led		
read	read		

These verbs end with /d/ or /t/ preceded by the free vowel /ii/. As with the verbs of group 3, the addition of a suffix /t/ appears as zero. However, there is the same change as in group 4a: free /ii/ is replaced by checked /ɛ/.

(c)

bite	bit
hide	hid
light	lit
slide	slid

The past participle of *bite* and *hide* are *bitten* and *hidden*, respectively; for *light* and *slide* the past participle is the same as the past tense, *lit* and *slid*, respectively. (For *light* there is also a /d/ suffix form, *lighted*.)

This group is analogous to the verbs of group 4b: the addition of /t/ shows up as a zero suffix but there is also a change of vowel, from free /ai/ to checked /ɪ/.

(d)

lose	lost
shoot	shot

Note what these two verbs have in common and what they share with the other verbs of 4a–c. They have in common a free vowel /uu/ in the simple form, changing to /ɒ/ in the past and participle. The form *lost* clearly has a suffixed /t/ and along with that there is voicing assimilation: /z/ → /s/ before /t/ (/luuz + t/ → /lɒst/). Since *shoot* ends with /t/, the /t/ suffix appears as zero.

Altogether we have accounted for the past tense (and, with two exceptions, the past participle) of the following verbs:

bend bet bite bleed breed build burn burst cast cost creep cut deal dream feed feel hide hit hurt keep kneel knit lead learn leave lend let light lose mean meet put quit read rid send set shed shoot shut sleep slide slit smell spell spend spill split spoil spread sweep thrust wed weep wet

All of these, we may say, add a basic suffix /t/, which occasions the following changes:

/t/ → 0 after /t/ and /d/   (*hit, spread*)
/d/ → 0 after /n/ or /l/ before /t/   (*bent, built*)

Free vowels are replaced by checked vowels, as follows:

/ii/ → /ɛ/   (*slept, fed*)
/ai/ → /ɪ/   (*bit*)

Voiced fricatives become voiceless before /t/:

/v/ → /f/   (*left*)
/z/ → /s/   (*lost*)

QUESTION 12.3

Which of the following verbs form the past tense with the /d/ suffix, which with the /t/ suffix, and which with either of them?

bereave cleave kneel leap speed

LOOKING BACK

Some morphemes – in fact, most morphemes – always occur as the same sequence of phonemes; *dog*, for instance, is pronounced the same in *birddog*, *doghouse*, and *doggie*. Some morphemes have variant forms called allomorphs. If every variable morpheme had its own kind of variation, listing these different variations would simply be an act of drudgery. Quite often, however, variable morphemes show the same kinds of variation, and recognizing these types of variation leads to a better understanding of what the language is like. A general statement about variation that is true in numerous instances – for example, a statement that a voiced obstruent changes to the corresponding voiceless one, or vice versa – is more insightful than a statement about /v/ changing to /f/ or vice versa.

An alternation is phonologically conditioned if a given phoneme (or sequence of phonemes) alternates with another phoneme (or sequence) under phonological conditions – the alternation depends on the kind of consonant or vowel or word boundary that precedes or follows, or on occurrence in a stressed syllable or an unstressed one. An alternation is morphologically conditioned if a given phoneme or sequence alternates with another phoneme or sequence under morphological conditions – the alternation occurs before a specific suffix or group of suffixes, for instance.

The first section of this chapter presented examples of palatalization and other kinds of assimilation, consonant cluster reduction, and vowel reduction, all of which occur under particular phonological conditions. The second section of the chapter dealt with morphologically conditioned alternations. The terms spirantization and velar softening (which originated with Chomsky and Halle 1968) refer, respectively, to a change of /t/ to /s/ and a change of /k/ to /s/ and /g/ to /ǰ/. These alternations are the result of phonetic changes that occurred long ago, in Greek and Late Latin; they apply only in words borrowed from those languages, which is a considerable part of the English vocabulary. The alternation of voiced and voiceless fricatives and the alternation of free vowels and checked vowels originated, for the most part, in English itself. Originally these alternations were purely phonological: voiced fricatives occurred only between voiced elements, and voiceless fricatives occurred in word-initial or word-final position or next to another voiceless consonant; checked vowels (originally short vowels) occurred before two consonants or before a coda of two syllables, and free vowels (originally long vowels) did not. But over the centuries other changes have obscured these simple kinds of conditions. Some of these phonological conditions are still evident but only to a limited degree.

Feedback on exercises

Some of the exercises have been invitations for readers to examine their own pronunciation, and these cannot have specific answers. Those that have definite answers, or possible answers, are discussed below.

2.1

1

	Articulator	*Point of articulation*
labiodental	lower lip	upper teeth
dorsovelar	dorsum (tongue-back)	velum (soft palate)
laminoalveolar	lamina (tongue-front)	alveolar ridge
centropalatal	tongue center	(hard) palate
apicodental	apex (tongue-tip)	upper teeth

2   end with a nasal: *doom*, *thumb*, *bang*;
begin with a fricative: *thumb*, *sand*, *shun*.

2.2

Higher	*Lower*	*Higher*	*Lower*
bit	bet	seat	sit
low	law	fate	fat
book	buck	Luke	look

3.2

Phonetic [sɛɫ kʰɪs stẽm]
Phonological /sænd tæp/

4.1

1   (a) voiced/voiceless   (d) voiced/voiceless
    (b) plosive/nasal   (e) plosive/fricative
    (c) plosive/fricative   (f) apical/laminal

2   /d/ voiced, /t/ voiceless
    /d/ plosive, /n/ nasal
    /d/ apical stop, /ǰ/ laminal affricate
    /d/ plosive, /ð/ fricative
    /d/ apical, /b/ labial
    /d/ apical, /g/ dorsal

3   /z/ zebra   /ǰ/ giant
    /k/ coral   /h/ whole
    /j/ yard   /ʃ/ shame
    /r/ write   /f/ phrase
    /w/ water   /ð/ though
    /s/ ceiling /g/ guest

4   /v/ never   /ð/ leather
    /ǰ/ pageant /č/ nature
    /θ/ method   /z/ reason
    /ŋ/ gingham /k/ ticket
    /ʒ/ measure /b/ robin
    /s/ listen   /ʃ/ patient

5.1

1   You should find slight – or not so slight – differences in the position of the tongue due to the fact that the dorsum is raised for *gig*, the apex for *did*, and neither for *bib*. Of course the tongue-front is high in all three words.

2 Assuming that you have a 'dark *l*' in post-vocalic position, the back of your tongue will be raised during part or all of the vowel. After the free vowels (*seal, fail, bowl, mile, owl*) /l/ may become – or tend to become – syllabic, [ḷ].

3 It is a general fact about English that vowels are longer before voiced consonants than before voiceless ones. In fact, sonorant consonants have the same variation in duration: /n/ is longer in *bend* than in *bent*, /l/ longer in *bulb* than in *gulp*.

5.2

1

/fɪʃ/	fish	/waif/	wife
/ʃiip/	sheep	/haus/	house
/čɛst/	chest	/joint/	joint
/grein/	grain	/pirs/	pierce
/blæk/	black	/sterz/	stairs
/pɑm/	palm	/gard/	guard
/kʊd/	could	/θɜrst/	thirst
/fruut/	fruit	/ʃur/	sure
/trʌmp/	trump	/porč/	porch
/houst/	host	/wɔrm/	warm
/θɔ/	thaw	/hair/	hire
/dɒk/	dock	/aur/	our, hour

2

Beth	/bɛθ/	these	/ðiiz/
patch	/pæč/	large	/larǰ/
brook	/brʊk/	stomp	/stɒmp/
crumb	/krʌm/	count	/kaunt/
third	/θɜrd/	goose	/guus/
noise	/noiz/	kind	/kaind/
dear	/dir/	gauze	/gɔz/
strict	/strɪkt/	quaint	/kweint/
phone	/foun/	storm	/stɔrm/

6.1

```
                    Word
            ┌─────────┴─────────┐
          Onset              Rhyme
                         ┌──────┴──────┐
                      Nucleus        Coda
         /dw             ɔ           (r)f/
         /gr            æ, ɑ          sp/
         /ǰ             ou            k/
         /pl             æ           ŋk/
         /skr           uu            o/
         /tr            ei           ps/
```

6.2

1   spr-   sprint, spray, spruce, spread, etc.
    sl-   slow, sled, slight, slumber, etc.
    ʃr-   shred, shrimp, shrewd, shrine, etc.
    θr-   three, thrifty, thrill, thrust, etc.
    tw-   twin, twice, tweezers, twist, etc.
    fl-   flat, flesh, flint, flutter, etc.
    skw-   square, squid, squall, squander

    -lθ   health, wealth, filth, tilth
    -nd   find, pound, expend, second, etc.
    -nǰ   hinge, lounge, avenge, lozenge, etc.
    -sk   desk, task, brisk, asterisk, etc.
    -ks   box, lax, annex, appendix, etc.
    -ps   lapse, ellipse, eclipse, traipse
    -lfθ   twelfth

2   Examples:

/-aip	-aib	-ait	-aid	-aič	-aiǰ	-aik	-aig/	
pipe	tribe	might	wide	0	oblige	like	0	
/-aif	-aiv	-ais	-aiz	-aiʃ	-aim	-ain	-aiŋ	-ail/
wife	drive	mice	wise	0	time	fine	0	mile
/-aimp	-aint	-aind	-aisp	-aist	-aisk	-ailb	-aild	-ailg/
0	pint	mind	0	Christ	0	0	wild	0
/-aup	-aub	-aut	-aud	-auč	-auǰ	-auk	-aug/	
0	0	out	loud	couch	gouge	0	0	
/-auf	-auv	-aus	-auz	-auʃ	-aum	-aun	-auŋ	-aul/
0	0	house	rouse	0	0	down	0	howl
/-aump	-aunt	-aund	-ausp	-aust	-ausk	-aulb	-auld	-aulg/
0	count	pound	0	roust	0	0	?	0

Some possible statements of constraint: /g/ and /ŋ/ do not occur after these free vowels (in fact, /ŋ/ does not occur after any free vowels and /g/ is rather rare after free vowels – *league, vague, fugue, rogue*); labial consonants do not occur after /au/; a cluster of two consonants after /ai/ and /au/ must be apical or laminal.

6.3

The suffix is /ɪz/ after *bridge, match, face, bush, rose, garage*; it is /s/ after *lip, hat, book, cuff, smith*; it is /z/ after *club, bed, egg, arm, tree, can, day, ring, toe, valve, lathe, bell, car.*

Rule

(a)   The regular plural suffix is pronounced /ɪz/ after sibilant consonants (/s z č ǰ ʃ ʒ/);

(b)   it is pronounced /s/ after other voiceless consonants (voiceless non-sibilant consonants /p t k f θ/);

(c)   it is pronounced /z/ after all other phonemes.

6.4

1   /ɪz/ after: Chris, Louise, Fish, Birch, the judge
     /s/ after: Hope, Robert, Dick, Ralph, Beth
     /z/ elsewhere

The rule is the same as for the regular plural.

2   /ɪz/ after: reach, budge, race, finish, raise, massage
     /s/ after: step, wait, look, laugh
     /z/ elsewhere

The rule is the same.

6.5

(a)   The regular past tense is pronounced /ɪd/ after verbs that end with /t/ or /d/ (*lift*, *need* in the list);

(b)   it is pronounced /t/ after other voiceless consonants (*hope*, *touch*, *cook*, *laugh*, *kiss*, *wish* in the list);

(c)   it is pronounced /d/ after all other phonemes.

7.1

Some possible ways of marking accent, stress, and other strong syllables:

(a)   We invíted them óver for ↓drínks.
(b)   Álison spént thrée yéars at ↓Stánford.
(c)   Ì can mánage thís jób by mỳ↓sélf.
(d)   Rúdy recéived a méssage from ↓Júdy.
(e)   Líttle Bò-Péep has lóst her ↓shéep.
(f)   Róme wàsn't búilt ìn a ↓dáy.
(g)   Dòn't cóunt your chíckens befóre thèy're ↓hátched.
(h)   Dòn't cróss the brídge befóre yòu ↓cóme tò it.
(i)   Pléase tùrn dówn the ↓thérmostàt.
(j)   Búsiness is fáirly ↓góod nów.

7.2

There are no right answers here. The crucial pair of words is *rushes* and *Russia's*. If you have /i/ in the second syllable of *rushes* and /ə/ in *Russia's*, you know which other words have /i/ and which have /ə/, in your speech. If *rushes* and *Russia's* are identical for you, you may have /i/ before laminal consonants (*polish*, *orange*, *sandwich*) and dorsal consonants (*ceiling*, *comic*, *hammock*) and /ə/ before other consonants.

8.1

1 (canóe): divide, forget, tonight
2 (sófa): breakfast, legal, magnet
3 (abándon): assemble, election, remember
4 (élephant): citizen, furniture, register
5 (humánity): apology, comedian, solicitous
6 (bàmbóo): campaign, cartoon, upstairs
7 (còntradíct): afternoon, convalesce, entertain
8 (télephòne): appetite, celebrate, longitude
9 (rèvolútion): democratic, exhibition, vaccination
10 (árchitècture): agriculture, communism, dandelion

8.2

1 Simple: *aspirin*; type 1: *postmark*; type 2: *bakery, colonial, hatred*; type 3: *telescope.*

2

annual	annuity	
S ww	w Sw w	
demolish	demolition	
w Sw	s wS w	
memorable	memorial	
S (w)w w	w S ww	
contribute	contribution	
w Sw	s wS w	
economy	economical	
wS w w	s w S ww	
admire	admirable	admiration
w S	S (w)w w	s wS w
allergy	allergic	allergenic
S w w	w S w	s w Sw
diplomat	diplomacy	diplomatic
S w s	w S ww	s w Sw
reside	resident	residential
w S	Sw w	s wS w

A weak syllable may be omitted, especially if followed by another weak syllable. Such an omission is noted here with '(w).' Note that the omission can create a consonant cluster /-dmr-/ that otherwise would not occur in an English word.

8.3

1   Noun and verb stressed differently:

contrast extract import overthrow progress project record subject survey

Noun and verb stressed alike (on the ult):

command control decay exchange supply surprise

There seems to be a growing tendency to stress some verbs in the first group like the corresponding nouns. Thus the verbs *contrast* and *extract*, especially, may be stessed on the first syllable by some speakers.

2   The verbs *omit* and *repel* do not follow the rule presented in this chapter, since they are stressed on the ult even though the ult, in both cases, contains a checked vowel followed by a single consonant. The noun *enamel* has a checked vowel in the penult with a single consonant following and thus, by our rules, should not be stressed on the penult, as it is. The words *ádversary* and *vóluntary*, if stressed as marked here, are irregular because both have a strong syllable before the ending *-ary*.

9.1

We may not all agree but the following are generally fore-stressed: *blood pressure, bottleneck, coffee cup, disease germ, homework, lifetime, light-year, oak tree, polar bear, soap suds, tear gas*; and the others are end-stressed.

9.2

1   These are generally end-stressed: *well-mannered, self-conscious, undernourished*; fore-stressed: *seasick, praiseworthy, poverty-stricken*; end-stressed in predicative position and fore-stressed in attributive position: *good-looking, easy-going, tax-free*.

2   Compound pronouns and the similar adverb compounds are fore-stressed. Reflexive pronouns are end-stressed except when a contrast is made.

9.3

íncome tax retùrn: a fore-stressed compound as the first part of a fore-stressed compound;

póst office clèrk: a fore-stressed compound as the first part of a fore-stressed compound;

sèeing-eye dóg: an end-stressed compound (*seeing éye*) as the first part of an end-stressed compound;

fìve-year plán: an end-stressed compound (*five yéar*) as the first part of an end-stressed compound;

mèdical technìcian tráining prògram: an end-stressed compound in which the first component is an end-stressed compound (*medical technícian*) and the second component is a fore-stressed compound (*tráining program*).

9.4

Of the three combinations of a verb + *on*, only *switch on* consists of verb + particle: *switch the lamp on*, *switch on the lamp*, *switch it on*.

10.1

Of the five utterances, the fourth is most likely to be a single tone unit. The first might be just one tone unit but it could equally well be two tone units. Divisions like the following are normal:

What this city needs | is better public transportation.
It needs much more than that, | I'd say.
First of all, | the police are underpaid.
The firemen need more modern equipment.
We don't have enough ambulances, | either.

Utterances divided more than this would perhaps suggest that the speaker is being very deliberate or is having difficulty in speaking.

10.2

Utterance 1a is unmarked. The speaker could be emphasizing the word *perfect* but not necessarily. There has to be an accented word in the utterance and the last word is accented unless there is reason for an earlier word to be accented. Utterance 1b says, in effect, that Manuel's English is not perfect, not really perfect, not absolutely perfect, etc. Paradigmatic focus puts the word *almost* in contrast with other words that might occur in the same position. Utterance 1c suggests that someone else's English has been mentioned previously. The name *Manuel* is contrasted with whatever name or names have been in the recent discourse.

Utterance 2a is a simple question, seeking information from the addressee; 2b would be likely if the addressee had just made a comment about not eating lunch in a particular place.

Utterance 3a informs us that Polly plays the flute as well as some other instrument that has just been named. 3b tells us that Polly, as well as some other person or persons, plays the flute.

In 4a the speaker seems to think the number mentioned before was *fourteen* and wants assurance of being right. Utterance 4b might be likely if the speaker needs assurance that it is *fourteen* and not some other number in the 'teens.'

Utterance 5a is 'normal'; deictic words like *us* and *here* are not accented unless there is contrast with other people or other places. Utterance 5b emphasizes that the presumed meeting should follow from Herbert's previous utterance. The interpretation of 5b would depend on the circumstances and one's knowledge of Herbert.

11.1

At least two of these vocal signals have a verbal equivalent. None of them has a universally accepted equivalent in a gestural form, but you may feel that there are such equivalents for some of the vocal signals, and we invite you to discuss the matter with others to see to what extent they agree. Our interpretation of the signals:

(a) a sound used to get the attention of someone not far away, usually in a situation where others are present and the person signaling wants to avoid undue attention;

(b) a conventional call for silence;

(c) a request for repetition or clarification; the equivalent of "↑What (did you say)?" but not the equivalent of "↓What?";

(d) an affirmative response; the equivalent of "Yes" in all the range of subtle meanings that can be signaled with that word;

(e) a conventional way of saying that one is cold or the weather is cold, and by extension a way of commenting on the lack of friendliness displayed by someone, which English also denotes as *cold*;

(f) a conventional means of commenting that someone's behavior or the situation that exists is not what it should be (especially when the situation in question is due to the actions or failure to act of one or more people); presumably, numerous repetitions of the signal would be a stronger statement than a few repetitions but we would really have to know the person signaling in order to interpret accurately.

11.2

1 A simple affirmative reply to a question would typically have a falling intonation: "Yes, it ↓ís." To refute what someone else has said (a negative statement) the accent would likely be on "Yes" with either falling or rising intonation: "↓Yés it is"; "↑Yés it is."

2 A rise on a question word ordinarily indicates a request for repetition or clarification: "↑Whén?" is essentially equivalent to "I know you mentioned a time but I didn't get it." A fall on a question word is a request for information that (the speaker believes) has not yet been communicated: "↓Whén?"

3 A rise–fall suggests a fairly strong show of interest, whether genuine or not. A short fall, on the other hand, would not be taken as encouragement to go on about the fishing trip. The fall–rise is like "No, but ... "; "No, but I have heard about ... "; "No, but I'll tell you about.... "

11.3

There are no right answers here. When interrupting, one might say something like "I'm ˇsórry." When people realize that they have just made a social mistake, "(Oh) °I'm ↘sórry" is not uncommon.

11.4

The following markings are appropriate but not the only possibilities.

1   The bus goes to ↗Clífton, ↗Ávonlea, ↗Hólly, and Fox ↓Híll.
2   Can you do me a ↑fávor? ˇMáybe.
3   We had a °great ↓tíme there.
4   To tell the ˇtrúth, | I'm °not at all im↘préssed.
5   Did you know she's won °three gold ↑médals? ˇThrée?

12.1

For most speakers, at least, *fiddler*, *juggler*, and *peddler* are /fidl- jʌgl- pɛdl-/ before the suffix /-ər/, and when no suffix follows the forms are /fɪdəl jʌgəl pɛdəl/. Thus /ə/ is inserted between a consonant and /l/ in final position because English words do not end with -cl. This insertion is exactly like the insertion of schwa between a consonant and final /r/ and, in fact, we should consider them instances of the same general rule: insert schwa between any consonant and a sonorant consonant in word-final position.

12.2

1   Comparing *completion*, *facial*, and *musician* with *complete*, *face*, and *music*, respectively, we observe that *face* ends with /s/; the /ʃ/ of facial results from the palatalization of this /s/ before -*ial*. The /t/ of *complete* becomes /s/ through spirantization, and then /s/ is changed to /ʃ/ before -*ion*. The change from /k/ in *music* to /ʃ/ in *musician* likewise requires two rules: velar softening /k → s/ and palatalization /s → ʃ/.
2   *ignite, suffice, vice.*

12.3

bereave: both /d/ suffix (*bereaved*) and /t/ suffix (*bereft*, like *left*);

cleave: /t/ suffix (*cleft*); also irregular forms *clove* for past tense and *cloven* for past participle; at any rate, not a common verb nowadays;

kneel: both /d/ (*kneeled*) and /t/ (*knelt*);

leap: both /d/ (*leaped*) and /t/ (*leapt*);

speed: both /d/ (*speeded*) and /t/ (*sped*).

Bibliography

Adams, Valerie. 1973. *An Introduction to Modern English Word-Formation*. London: Longman.

Allerton, D.J. 1978. "The notion of 'givenness' and its relation to presupposition and to theme." *Lingua*, 34: 1–29.

Anderson, John M., and Ewen, Colin J. 1987. *Principles of Dependency Phonology*. Cambridge: Cambridge University Press.

Anderson, Stephen R. 1985. *Phonology in the Twentieth Century: Theories of Rules and Theories of Representations*. Chicago: University of Chicago Press.

Arnold, G.F. 1957. "Stress in English words." *Lingua*, 6: 221–67.

Bailey, Charles-James N. 1980. Evidence for variable syllable boundaries in English. In L.R. Waugh and C.H. Schooneveld (eds) *The Melody of Language*. Baltimore: University Park Press, 25–39.

Bailey, Richard W., and Görlach, Manfred (eds). 1982. *English as a World Language*. Ann Arbor: University of Michigan Press.

Bauer, Laurie. 1983. *English Word Formation*. Cambridge: Cambridge University Press.

Bell, Alan, and Hooper, Joan Bybee (eds). 1978. *Syllables and Segments*. Amsterdam: North Holland.

Berger, Marshall D. 1968. "Accent, pattern, and dialect in North American English." *Word*, 24: 55–61.

Bickerton, Derek. 1990. *Language and Species*. Chicago: University of Chicago Press.

Bing, Janet M. 1985. *Aspects of English Prosody*. New York and London: Garland.

Bolinger, Dwight L. 1958. "A theory of word accent in English." *Word*, 14: 109–48.

—— 1961. "Contrastive accent and contrastive stress." *Language*, 37: 83–96.

—— 1986. *Intonation and its Parts: Melody in Spoken English*. Stanford, CA: Stanford University Press.

Brazil, David, Coulthard, Malcolm, and Johns, Catherine. 1980. *Discourse, Intonation and Language Teaching*. London: Longman.

Brown, Gillian. 1990. *Listening to Spoken English*. 2nd edn. Harlow: Longman.

Brown, Gillian, Currie, Karen L., and Kenworthy, Joanne. 1980. *Questions of Intonation*. Baltimore: University Park Press.

Burzio, Luigi. 1994. *Principles of English Stress*. Cambridge: Cambridge University Press.

Catford, J.C. 1988. *A Practical Course in Phonetics*. Oxford: Clarendon Press.

Chafe, Wallace. 1994. *Discourse, Consciousness, and Time: the Flow and Displacement of Conscious Experience in Speaking and Writing*. Chicago: University of Chicago Press.

Chomsky, Noam. 1995. *The Minimalist Program*. Cambridge, MA: MIT Press.

Chomsky, Noam, and Halle, Morris. 1968. *The Sound Pattern of English*. New York: Harper & Row.

Clark, Herbert H., and Clark, Eve V. 1977. *Psychology and Language: an Introduction to Psycholinguistics*. New York: Harcourt Brace Jovanovich.

Clark, John, and Yallop, Colin. 1995. *An Introduction to Phonetics and Phonology*. 2nd edn. Oxford: Blackwell.

Couper-Kuhlen, Elizabeth. 1986. *An Introduction to English Prosody*. London: Edward Arnold.

Cruttenden, Alan. 1986. *Intonation*. Cambridge: Cambridge University Press.

Crystal, David A. 1969. *Prosodic Systems and Intonation in English*. Cambridge: Cambridge University Press.

—— 1991. *A Dictionary of Linguistics and Phonetics*. 3rd edn. Oxford: Blackwell.

—— 1995. *The Cambridge Encyclopedia of the English Language*. Cambridge: Cambridge University Press.

Crystal, David, and Quirk, Randolph. 1964. *Systems of Prosodic and Paralinguistic Features in English*. The Hague: Mouton.

Daneš, Frantisek. 1960. "Sentence intonation from a functional point of view." *Word*, 16: 34–54.

Dickerson, Wayne. 1975. "Predicting word stress: generative rules in an ESL context." *TESL Studies*, l: 38–52.

Fallows, Deborah. 1981. "Experimental evidence for English syllabification and syllable structure." *Journal of Linguistics*, 17: 309–17.

Fudge, Erik. 1975. "English word stress: an examination of some basic assumptions." In D.L. Goyvaerts and G.K. Pullum (eds) *Essays on the Sound Pattern of English*. Ghent: Story-Scientia, 277–323.

—— 1984. *English Word Stress*. London: Allen & Unwin.

Giegerich, Heinz J. 1992. *English Phonology: an Introduction*. Cambridge: Cambridge University Press.

Gimson, A.C. 1994. *An Introduction to the Pronunciation of English*. 5th edn, revised by A. Cruttenden. London: Edward Arnold/New York: St. Martin's Press.

Goldsmith, John. 1990. *Autosegmental and Metrical Phonology*. Oxford: Blackwell.

Goyvaerts, D.L., and Pullum, G.K. (eds). 1975. *Essays on the Sound Pattern of English*. Ghent: Story-Scientia.

Gulden, Brigitte K. 1985. *The Secret of Sounding Native: a Phonological Analysis of Proclitics in North American English*. (European University Studies, Series XIV, Vol. 14.) Frankfurt on Main: Peter Lang.

Halle, Morris. 1973. "Stress rules in English: a new version." *Linguistic Inquiry*, 4: 451–64.

Halle, Morris, and Clements, George N. 1982. *Problem Book in Phonology: a Workbook for Introductory Courses in Linguistics and in Modern Phonology*. Cambridge, MA: MIT Press.

Halle, Morris, and Keyser, Samuel Jay. 1971. *English Stress: its Form, its Growth, and its Role in Verse*. New York: Harper & Row.

Halle, Morris, and Mohanan, K.P. 1985. "Segmental phonology of modern English." *Linguistic Inquiry*, 16: 57–116.

Halle, Morris, and Vergnaud, Roger. 1987. *An Essay on Stress*. Cambridge, MA: MIT Press.

Halliday, M.A.K. 1967. *Intonation and Grammar in British English*. The Hague: Mouton.

—— 1970. *A Course in Spoken English: Intonation*. London: Oxford University Press.

—— 1989. *Spoken and Written Language*. Oxford: Oxford University Press.

Halliday, M.A.K., and Hasan, Ruqaiya. 1976. *Cohesion in English*. London: Longman.

Harris, John. 1994. *English Sound Structure*. Oxford: Blackwell.

Hayes, Bruce. 1995. *Metrical Stress Theory: Principles and Case Studies*. Chicago: University of Chicago Press.

Hockett, Charles F. 1955. *Manual of Phonology*. (*International Journal of American Linguistics*, Memoir 11.)

—— 1958. *A Course in Modern Linguistics*. New York: Macmillan.

Hogg, Richard, and McCully, C.B. 1987. *Metrical Phonology: a Coursebook*. Cambridge: Cambridge University Press.

Hubbell, Allen F. 1950. *The Pronunciation of English in New York City: Consonants and Vowels*. New York: Kings Crown Press.

Hughes, Arthur, and Trudgill, Peter. 1987. *English Accents and Dialects*. 2nd edn. London: Edward Arnold.

Hyman, Larry. 1975. *Phonology: Theory and Analysis*. New York: Holt, Rinehart, & Winston.

Jensen, John T. 1993. *English Phonology*. Amsterdam and Philadelphia: John Benjamins.

Jones, Daniel. 1976. *An Outline of English Phonetics*. 9th edn. Cambridge: Cambridge University Press.

—— 1977. *Everyman's Pronouncing Dictionary, Containing over 58,000 Words in International Phonetic Transcription*. 14th edn, edited by A. C. Gimson. London: Dent.

Kachru, Braj B. 1986. *The Alchemy of English*. Oxford: Pergamon.

Kahn, Daniel. 1976. *Syllable-based Generalizations in English Phonology*. Bloomington: Indiana University Linguistics Club.

Katamba, Francis. 1989. *An Introduction to Phonology*. Harlow: Longman.

Kenyon, John S., and Knott, Thomas A. 1953. *A Pronouncing Dictionary of American English*. Springfield, MA: Merriam.

Kingdon, Roger. 1958a *The Groundwork of English Stress*. London: Longman.

—— 1958b. *The Groundwork of English Intonation*. London: Longman.

Klavans, Judith L. 1985. "The independence of syntax and phonology in cliticization." *Language*, 61: 95–120.

Kreidler, Charles W. 1972a. "English orthography: a generative approach." In James E. Alatis (ed.) *Studies in Honor of Albert H. Marckwardt*. Washington: Teachers of English to Speakers of Other Languages, 81–91.

—— 1972b. "Teaching English spelling and pronunciation." *TESOL Quarterly*, 5: 3–12.

—— 1984. "The uses of accent in English sentences." *SECOL Review*, 8: 9–27.

—— 1987. "Stress differentiation in sets of English words." *Word*, 38: 99–126.

—— 1989. *The Pronunciation of English: a Coursebook in Phonology*. Oxford: Blackwell.

—— 1990. "Toward a pan-dialect phonology of English." *Word*, 41: 69–80.

Kurath, Hans. 1967. *A Phonology and Prosody of Modern English*. Ann Arbor: University of Michigan Press.

Kurath, Hans, and McDavid, Raven I., Jr. 1961. *The Pronunciation of English in the Atlantic States*. Ann Arbor: University of Michigan Press.

Ladd, D. Robert. 1980. *The Structure of Intonational Meaning*. Bloomington: Indiana University Press.

Ladefoged, Peter. 1962. *Elements of Acoustic Phonetics*. Chicago: University of Chicago Press.

—— 1993. *A Course in Phonetics*. 3rd edn. Fort Worth, TX: Harcourt Brace Jovanovich.

Lass, Roger. 1984. *Phonology: an Introduction to Basic Concepts*. Cambridge: Cambridge University Press.

—— 1987. *The Shape of English: Structure and History*. London: Dent.

Leben, William R. 1976. "The tones in English intonation." *Linguistic Analysis*, 2: 69–107.

Lehiste, Ilse. 1970. *Suprasegmentals*. Cambridge, MA: MIT Press.

Lencho, Mark W. 1989. *A Grid-Based Theory of Stress in English: a Revised Account*. Bloomington: Indiana University Linguistics Club.

Liberman, Mark, and Prince, Alan. 1977. "On stress and linguistic rhythm." *Linguistic Inquiry*, 8: 249–336.

Lieberman, Philip. 1977. *Speech Physiology and Acoustic Phonetics*. New York: Macmillan.

Lightner, T.M. 1972. *Problems in the Theory of Phonology*, Vol. 1. Edmonton: Linguistic Research.

Lyons, John. 1968. *Introduction to Theoretical Linguistics*. Cambridge: Cambridge University Press.

—— 1995. *Linguistic Semantics: an Introduction*. Cambridge: Cambridge University Press.

McArthur, Tom (ed.). 1992. *The Oxford Companion to the English Language*. Oxford and New York: Oxford University Press.

McConnell, R.E. 1979. *Our Own Voice: Canadian English and How it is Studied*. Toronto: Gage.

Makkai, Valerie Becker (ed.). 1972. *Phonological Theory: Evolution and Current Practice*. New York: Holt, Rinehart, & Winston.

Marchand, Hans. 1969. *The Categories and Types of Present-Day English Word-Formation*. 2nd edn. Munich: C.H. Beck.

Milroy, J. 1981. *Regional Accents of English: Belfast*. Belfast: Blackstaff Press.

Mohanan, K.P. 1986. *The Theory of Lexical Phonology*. Dordrecht: Reidel.

O'Connor, J.D. 1973. *Phonetics*. Harmondsworth: Penguin.

O'Connor, J.D., and Arnold, G.F. 1973. *Intonation of Colloquial English: a Practical Handbook*. 2nd edn. London: Longman.

O'Connor, J.D., and Trim, J.L.M. 1953. "Vowel, consonant, and syllable: a phonological definition." *Word*, 9: 103–22.

Palmer, Harold, and Blandford, F.G. 1976. *A Grammar of Spoken English*. 3rd. edn, revised and rewritten by Roger Kingdon. Cambridge: Cambridge University Press.

Pierrehumbert, Janet Breckenridge. 1987. *The Phonology and Phonetics of English Intonation*. Bloomington, IN: Indiana University Linguistics Club.

Pike, Kenneth L. 1945. *The Intonation of American English*. Ann Arbor: University of Michigan Press.

Pinker, Steven. 1994. *The Language Instinct: How the Mind Creates Language*. New York: William Morrow.

Platt, J.T., Weber, H., and Ho, M.L. 1984. *The New Englishes*. London: Routledge & Kegan Paul.

Poldauf, Ivan. 1984. *English Word Stress: a Theory of Word-Stress in English*. Oxford: Pergamon.

Roach, Peter. 1991. *English Phonetics and Phonology: a Practical Course*. 2nd edn. Cambridge: Cambridge University Press.

Roberts, P.A. *West Indians and their Language*. Cambridge: Cambridge University Press.

Romaine, Suzanne. 1988. *Pidgin and Creole Languages*. London: Longman.

Schane, Sanford A. 1975. "Noncyclic English word stress." In D.L. Goyvaerts and G.K. Pullum (eds) *Essays on the Sound Pattern of English*. Ghent: Story-Scientia, 249–59.

Selkirk, Elizabeth. 1980. *The Phrase Phonology of English and French*. New York: Garland.

—— 1984. *Phonology and Syntax: the Relation between Sound and Structure*. Cambridge, MA: MIT Press.

Sherman, Donald. 1975. "Noun–verb stress alternation: an example of the lexical diffusion of sound change in English." *Linguistics*, 159: 43–71.

Sommerstein, Alan. 1977. *Modern Phonology*. London: Edward Arnold.

Spencer, Andrew. 1996. *Phonology: Theory and Description*. Oxford: Blackwell.

Stenberg, Martha. 1988. *Os elementos não-verbais da conversação*. São Paulo: Atual.

Tench, Paul. 1990. *The Roles of Intonation in English Discourse*. (Forum Linguisticum, Vol. 31.) Frankfurt on Main: Peter Lang.

Thompson, Henry S. 1981. *Stress and Salience in English: Theory and Practice*. Palo Alto, CA: Xerox.

Trager, George L., and Smith, Henry Lee, Jr. 1951. *Outline of English Structure*. (Studies in Linguistics, Occasional Papers 3.)

Trubetzkoy, N.S. 1931. "Phonologie et géographie linguistique." *Travaux du Cercle Linguistique de Prague*, 4: 228–34.

Trudgill, Peter (ed.). 1984. *Language in the British Isles*. Cambridge: Cambridge University Press.

—— 1986. *Dialects in Contact*. Oxford: Blackwell.

—— 1990. *The Dialects of England*. Oxford: Blackwell.

Trudgill, Peter, and Hannah, Jean. 1994. *International English: a Guide to Varieties of Standard English*. 3rd edn. London: Edward Arnold.

Turner, G.W. 1966. *The English Language in Australia and New Zealand*. London: Longman.

Vanderslice, Ralph, and Ladefoged, Peter. 1972. "Binary suprasegmental features and transformational word-accentuation rules." *Language*, 48: 819–38.

Walker, John. 1791. *A Critical Pronouncing Dictionary*. London: Robinson. Facsimile reprint. Menston: Scolar Press. 1968.

Wardhaugh, Ronald. 1993. *Investigating Language: Central Problems in Linguistics*. Oxford: Blackwell.

Wells, J.C. 1982. *Accents of English*. 3 vols. Cambridge: Cambridge University Press.

—— 1990. *Longman Pronouncing Dictionary*. Harlow: Longman.

Wijk, Axel. 1966. *Rules of Pronunciation for the English Language*. London: Oxford University Press.

Willems, Nico. 1982. *English Intonation from a Dutch Point of View*. Dordrecht: Foris.

Wolfram, Walt, and Johnson, Robert. 1982. *Phonological Analysis: Focus on American English*. Washington: Center for Applied Linguistics.

Index

accent 11, 102–8, 121, 141,
    162–74; mobile accent 105
Adams, V. 159
adjective 103, 106, 135–42,
    149–50
adjective compound 146–52
adjective phrase 149
adverb compound 151–2
adverbial phrase 150
affix 132; neutral 132
affricate 50, 52, 54, 62
allomorph 97–9, 100
allophones 40, 42, 56
alphabet 86
alternation 196–211;
    morphologically
    conditioned 200–5, 210;
    phonologically
    conditioned 197–9, 210;
    voiced/voiceless 202–3;
    vowel 204–5
alveolar ridge 20, 52
ambiguity 165–6
America, American 68, 75,
    76, 78, 81
American English 7, 105
amplitude 15
anaphora, anaphoric 170–3,
    175–6; grammatical 173,
    175–6; lexical 173, 175–6
Anguilla 6

antepenult 136–40
Antigua 6
apex 20, 52
apical groove 57
apicoalveolar 21
apicodental 21
appearance 179
Arnold, G. 142, 193
articulated 18
articulation: manner of
    18–20; place of 20–1, 23,
    31
articulator 20
aspirated 38, 58
assimilation 102, 116–19;
    mutual 118; progressive
    116–17, 119; regressive 116
Australia 6, 68, 72, 73, 77, 81,
    119
auxiliary (verb) 111–12, 117,
    155, 174

back-formation 155
Bahamas 6
Bailey, R. 10
Bangladesh 7
Barbados 6
base 132
Bauer, L. 159
Belize 6
Bermuda 6

bilabial 21
Bing, J. 193
Birmingham 4
Bolinger, D. 193
bound morpheme *see* morpheme
British Broadcasting Corporation 4
British dialects, British English 68,
    105
Broad Australian 6, 74, 75
Brown, G. 193
Burzio, L. 142

/č/ 59
Cameroon 7
Canada, Canadian 5, 68, 72, 75, 76,
    81
cardinal vowel 26–8, 31–2
Caribbean 6, 68, 74, 82
centering diphthong 81
centropalatal 21
checked vowel 71–2, 80, 83, 88, 100
Chomsky, N. 142, 210
Clark, E. 48
Clark, H. 48
Clark, J. 32
clause 164; restrictive,
    non-restrictive 165
clear /l/ 43, 57
Cockney 4, 74, 75, 81
coda of syllable 87–9, 92–6, 98–100;
    of tone unit 168, 171; of
    utterance 187–91; of word 125–8,
    141
commutation 146
complement 145, 149, 155
complementary distribution 61
complex word 132
complexity in vowels 70
composite word 131; three types of
    131–3
compound tunes 187–91
compound word 131; *see also*
    adjective compound; adverb
    compound; noun compound;
    verb compound
conjunction 146
consonant 17–26; cluster 90–100;
    loss 114–15; obstruent 17–18, 50,
    91; sonorant 19
constraint on phoneme occurrence
    88–95, 100
contraction 115, 117–18

Couper-Kuhlen, E. 193
Cruttenden, A. 193
Crystal, D. 10, 193
Currie, K. 193

dark /l/ 43, 57–8
Delaware 6
deletion of consonant 197; of vowel
    97
determiner 111
dialect 2–4, 66–8, 70–2, 83
diaphragm 16
Dickerson, W. 142
differences in vocabulary 8; in
    morphology 8; in syntax 8
diphthong 70
discourse, spoken and written 34–5,
    167; role of accent 162–72
distinctive feature 48, 50–4,
    56–61
Dominica 6
dorsopalatal 21
dorsovelar 21
dorsum 20
duration 29
Dutch 83

egressive lung air 16, 31
either 165
endocentric compound 146
end-stress 145–57
England 5–7, 72, 74, 77, 78, 81
exocentric compound 147
expansion 146

fall–rise 183–5, 192
falling tunes 178, 181–3, 184–5
feature: distinctive, non-distinctive
    48, 50, 56–61; phonetic 18;
    prosodic 29
Florida 6
foot, metrical 128–30
fore-stress 145–57
free morpheme *see* morpheme
free variation 61
free vowel 71, 80, 83, 88, 100
French 105
frequency of vibration 15, 178
fricative 19, 23–5, 31, 50–4, 60; flat
    51; glottal 16; sibilant 52–4
Fudge, E. 142, 159
function word 103, 107–8

Gambia 7
Ghana 7
General American 6
generic name 148
German 83
gestures 179
Gimson, A. 120
Glasgow 3
glide 50–l, 54, 91–2, 93; glottal 50; oral 50
glottal fricative 16
glottal stop 16
glottalized plosives 59
glottis 16
Görlach, M. 10
grammar 9
grammatical meaning 96
graphic unit 86
Great Lakes 6
Greek 199, 211
Grenada 6
Guyana 6

Halle, M. 142, 210
Halliday, M. 176, 193
Hannah, J. 10
has 115–16
Hayes, B. 142
he 171
head of noun phrase 145
high onset 186–7
Ho, M. 11
Hockett, C. 32
Hogg, R. 142
homophonous suffixes 114
Hong Kong 7

incidence 67
India 7
inflection 96–9
inflectional suffix 96
intensity 29
intercostal muscles 16
intonation 8, 163
intransitive verb compound 156
introductory remark 164
intrusive R 79
inventory 67–73, 80–2
Ireland, Irish 5, 68, 72, 74, 75, 77, 78, 80
Irish Gaelic 5

is 115–16
it 171

Jamaica 6, 82
Jones, D. 120

Kachru, B. 11
Katamba, F. 48
Kenworthy, J. 193
Kenya 7
Kingdon, R. 142, 193
Kreidler, C. 84, 142

/l/ 51, 54, 57–8
labial 53–4, 60
labiodental 21, 23
Ladefoged, P. 32, 62, 100, 120
lamina 20–1
laminoalveolar 21, 23
larynx 16–17
Lass, R. 62
lateral 24–5, 51
Latin 199, 211
length 70
lexical meaning 35
lexical word 103
Liberia 7
Liberman, M. 142
linking R 79
lips 20–1; shape (rounded, spread) 42, 56
liquid 50, 54, 60
Liverpool 3, 4
London 4
long fall 181, 192
long rise 182–3, 185, 192
low onset 186–7
lungs 16–17
Lyons, J. 193

McArthur, T. 10
McCully, C. 142
Malaysia 7
Malawi 7
Manchester 4
Mandarin Chinese 30
manner of articulation 18–20
Marchand, H. 159
Maryland 6
merger of phonemes 68
metrical foot 128
Metrical Phonology 128–30, 142

Midland dialect area 6
minimal pairs 45
modifier 145
monophthong 70
Monserrat 6
morpheme 35, 62, 131–3, 144
morphological conditioning 200–5
morphological structure 130–4
morphology 8, 9
mutual assimilation 118
mutual influence 57
mutually intelligible 36

/ŋ/ 62
nasal cavity 17
nasal consonants 19, 21, 23
nasal phonemes 39, 50, 52–4, 56
nasalized tap 59
nasalized vowels 41–2
neutral affix 132
neutral occurrence of accent 168
neutralization of contrast 46
Nevis 6
New Brunswick 5
New England 6, 72, 78
New Jersey 6
New York 6
New Zealand 7, 68, 72, 73, 77, 81
Newfoundland 5
Nigeria 7
non-rhotic 72, 77–9
Norman Conquest 5
North America(n) 5, 59, 75, 77–8,
    81
North of England 3
Northern Ireland 5, 76, 80
Northern USA 6
Norwich 4
not 117
noun 103–4, 106, 111, 135–42, 149,
    155
noun compound 144–9
noun phrase 103–4, 111, 144–9, 151,
    167
Nova Scotia 5
nuclear syllable 125–6
nucleus of syllable 87–90, 99–100; of
    tone unit 168, 71; of utterance
    187–91; of word 125–8, 141

obstruent consonant 17–20, 50, 56,
    58, 91

O'Connor, J. 193
one(s) 172
onset of syllable 86–92; of tone unit
    168, 171; of utterance 187–91; of
    word 125–8, 141
oral cavity 17

Pakistan 7
palatalization 118, 200–2
palate 20–1, 52
paradigmatic focus 169–70
paralanguage 8, 178–80
particle 147, 156–8
past tense suffix 96–9, 206–9
Pennsylvania 6
penult 107, 136–40
pharynx 17–20
Philadelphia 3
Philippines 7
phone 16–28
phoneme 38–46, 66–8
phonetic norm 69
phonetic realization 67
phonetic weakening 112
phonetics 16
phonological conditioning 197–9
phonology 9, 41
phrase 149
Pierrehumbert, J. 193
Pike, K. 193
Pinker, S. 10
pitch 14
place name 146, 148
place of articulation 20–1
Platt, J. 11
plosive 19–23, 50–4, 56, 58
plural suffix 96–9, 116
Poldauf, I. 142
possessive suffix 96–9, 111
pre-antepenult 136
prefix 132
preposition 107–8, 111–24, 146, 151,
    156–8
prepositional phrase 104, 151
Prince, A. 142
Prince Edward Island 5
progressive assimilation 116
pronoun 107–8, 111
pronunciation 66–7
prosodic feature 29–30
prosody 36, 163–74
proxemics 179

qualifier 149–50
quality of vowel 26, 69
question word 182–3

/r/ 54, 63
R-vowel 72–3, 77–9, 80–2
radicopharyngeal 21
radix 20
Received Pronunciation (RP) 4,
    75–8, 82
release of plosive 58–9
resonance 91
rhotic 72
rhyme, syllable 88, 90; word 125
rise–fall 184–5
Roach, P. 62, 100, 120

St Kitts 6
St Lucia 6
St Vincent 6
scale of sonority 91
schwa 109–10
Scotland, Scots 5, 68, 72, 74–8, 80
Scots Gaelic 5
sentence 104
sentence stress 121
she 171
short fall 181–5, 192
short rise 183–5, 192
sibilant 25, 51–2, 54
Sierra Leone 7
silent E 203
simple tone unit 180–7
simple word 131, 146
Singapore 7
Smith, H. 120
some 172
sonorant consonant 18–20, 50, 56–7,
    91
sound 14–15
South Africa 7, 68, 72, 81
Southern UK 3
Southern USA 6
specific name 148
spirantization 200–1
split 67
Sri Lanka 7
standard 4
stop 50
stress 102–8, 124–40, 145
strong penult 105
strong syllable 105–8, 126–8

suffix 132–4, 136–40, 206–9
superordinate term 173
syllabic /r l n m/ 110–11
syllabic timing 103
syllable 29–30, 37, 102–14, 124–30
synonym 173
syntagmatic focus 168–71
syntax 8, 9

Tanzania 6
tapped /t d/ 59
teeth 20–1, 52, 56
they 171
third-person singular suffix 98,
    116
tick 120
tonality 163–6
tone 14, 29–30
tone unit 37, 162–71, 178, 180–7
tongue 18, 20, 51–4, 56–7, 70; shape
    of 24–5, 57
tonicity 163, 166–71
too 165
trachea 16–17
Trager, G. 120
transitive verb compound 156–7
tree diagrams 128–9
Trinidad and Tobago 6
triphthong 70
Trudgill, P. 10, 11
tune 178; compound 187–91
type 2 and type 3 suffixes 133–5
types of composite word 131–3

Uganda 7
Ulster 5
ult 136–7, 140
United Kingdom 5, 73
United States 5, 72
utterance 35, 162–4

Vanderslice, R. 120
variation 2–9; in weak syllables
    112–18
velar softening 201–2, 210–11
velum 19–21, 52
verb 104, 106, 111, 135–42, 149, 155
verb compound 154–8
verb phrase 104, 154–5
verbal, non-verbal 179–80
Vergnaud, R. 142
vibration 14–15, 18, 30–1

Virgin Islands 6
vocabulary differences 8
vocal, non-vocal 179–80
vocal cords 16
vocal tract 16–17
vocative 165
voice onset time 53
voiced, voiceless 21–5, 53–4, 59
voiceless onset 57–8
voiceless plosive 58–9
voicing 21–4
vowel 26–8, 69–84; free, checked 71–2, 80, 83, 88, 100
vowel alternation 204–5, 211
vowel insertion 197–8
vowel loss 115–16, 119–20
vowel reduction 112–13, 119–20

Wales, Welsh 5, 72, 77
Walker, J. 142
Wardhaugh, R. 10
Weber, H. 11
Wells, J. 10, 84
WH-question 183
word 35–6
word rhyme 125
writing 162–3

Yallop, C. 32
yes–no question 182

Zambia 7
zero 172
Zimbabwe 7
/ʒ/ 62